1994

fan Tutte • Die Zauberflöte • Boris Godunov • La Bohème • Tosca • Madama Butterfly • Turandot • Il Barbiere di Siviglia • Die Fledern
Nibelungen • Das Rheingold • Die Walküre • Siegfried • Götterdämmerung • Fidelio • Norma • Car
na Butterfly • Turandot • Il Barbiere di Siviglia • Die Fledermaus • Der Rosenkavalier • Rigoletto • I
kavalier • Rigoletto • Il Trovatore • La Traviata • Aida • Otello • Falstaff • Tristan und Isolde •
I Pagliacci • Cavalleria Rusticana • Le Nozze di Figaro • Don Giovanni • Così fan Tutte • Die Zauberflöte • Boris Godunov • La Bohème
ello • Falstaff • Tristan und Isolde • Die Meistersinger von Nürnberg • Der Ring des Nibelungen • Das Rheingold • Die Walküre • S
on Giovanni • Così fan Tutte • Die Zauberflöte • Boris Godunov • La Bohème • Tosca • Madama Butterfly • Turandot • Il Barbiere di Sivi
g • Der Ring des Nibelungen • Das Rheingold • Die Walküre • Siegfried • Götterdämmerung • Fidelio • Norma • Carmen • Lucia di Lamn
ème • Tosca • Madama Butterfly • Turandot • Il Barbiere di Siviglia • Die Fledermaus • Der Rosenkavalier • Rigoletto • Il Trovatore • La
Götterdämmerung • Fidelio • Norma • Carmen • Lucia di Lammermoor • Porgy and Bess • I Pagliacci • Cavalleria Rusticana • Le Nozze c
dermaus • Der Rosenkavalier • Rigoletto • Il Trovatore • La Traviata • Aida • Otello • Falstaff • Tristan und Isolde • Die Meistersinger von
and Bess • I Pagliacci • Cavalleria Rusticana • Le Nozze di Figaro • Don Giovanni • Così fan Tutte • Die Zauberflöte • Boris Godunov • La
Otello • Falstaff • Tristan und Isolde • Die Meistersinger von Nürnberg • Der Ring des Nibelungen • Das Rheingold • Die Walküre • S
on Giovanni • Così fan Tutte • Die Zauberflöte • Boris Godunov • La Bohème • Tosca • Madama Butterfly • Turandot • Il Barbiere di Sivi
g • Der Ring des Nibelungen • Das Rheingold • Die Walküre • Siegfried • Götterdämmerung • Fidelio • Norma • Carmen • Lucia di Lamn
ème • Tosca • Madama Butterfly • Turandot • Il Barbiere di Siviglia • Die Fledermaus • Der Rosenkavalier • Rigoletto • Il Trovatore • La
Götterdämmerung • Fidelio • Norma • Carmen • Lucia di Lammermoor • Porgy and Bess • I Pagliacci • Cavalleria Rusticana • Le Nozze c
dermaus • Der Rosenkavalier • Rigoletto • Il Trovatore • La Traviata • Aida • Otello • Falstaff • Tristan und Isolde • Die Meistersinger von
and Bess • I Pagliacci • Cavalleria Rusticana • Le Nozze di Figaro • Don Giovanni • Così fan Tutte • Die Zauberflöte • Boris Godunov • La
Otello • Falstaff • Tristan und Isolde • Die Meistersinger von Nürnberg • Der Ring des Nibelungen • Das Rheingold • Die Walküre • S
on Giovanni • Così fan Tutte • Die Zauberflöte • Boris Godunov • La Bohème • Tosca • Madama Butterfly • Turandot • Il Barbiere di Sivi
g • Der Ring des Nibelungen • Das Rheingold • Die Walküre • Siegfried • Götterdämmerung • Fidelio • Norma • Carmen • Lucia di Lamn
ème • Tosca • Madama Butterfly • Turandot • Il Barbiere di Siviglia • Die Fledermaus • Der Rosenkavalier • Rigoletto • Il Trovatore • La
Götterdämmerung • Fidelio • Norma • Carmen • Lucia di Lammermoor • Porgy and Bess • I Pagliacci • Cavalleria Rusticana • Le Nozze d
dermaus • Der Rosenkavalier • Rigoletto • Il Trovatore • La Traviata • Aida • Otello • Falstaff • Tristan und Isolde • Die Meistersinger von
and Bess • I Pagliacci • Cavalleria Rusticana • Le Nozze di Figaro • Don Giovanni • Così fan Tutte • Die Zauberflöte • Boris Godunov • La
Otello • Falstaff • Tristan und Isolde • Die Meistersinger von Nürnberg • Der Ring des Nibelungen • Das Rheingold • Die Walküre • S
on Giovanni • Così fan Tutte • Die Zauberflöte • Boris Godunov • La Bohème • Tosca • Madama Butterfly • Turandot • Il Barbiere di Sivi
g • Der Ring des Nibelungen • Das Rheingold • Die Walküre • Siegfried • Götterdämmerung • Fidelio • Norma • Carmen • Lucia di Lamn
ème • Tosca • Madama Butterfly • Turandot • Il Barbiere di Siviglia • Die Fledermaus • Der Rosenkavalier • Rigoletto • Il Trovatore • La
Götterdämmerung • Fidelio • Norma • Carmen • Lucia di Lammermoor • Porgy and Bess • I Pagliacci • Cavalleria Rusticana • Le Nozze d
dermaus • Der Rosenkavalier • Rigoletto • Il Trovatore • La Traviata • Aida • Otello • Falstaff • Tristan und Isolde • Die Meistersinger von
and Bess • I Pagliacci • Cavalleria Rusticana • Le Nozze di Figaro • Don Giovanni • Così fan Tutte • Die Zauberflöte • Boris Godunov • La
Otello • Falstaff • Tristan und Isolde • Die Meistersinger von Nürnberg • Der Ring des Nibelungen • Das Rheingold • Die Walküre • S
on Giovanni • Così fan Tutte • Die Zauberflöte • Boris Godunov • La Bohème • Tosca • Madama Butterfly • Turandot • Il Barbiere di Sivi
g • Der Ring des Nibelungen • Das Rheingold • Die Walküre • Siegfried • Götterdämmerung • Fidelio • Norma • Carmen • Lucia di Lamm
ème • Tosca • Madama Butterfly • Turandot • Il Barbiere di Siviglia • Die Fledermaus • Der Rosenkavalier • Rigoletto • Il Trovatore • La T
Götterdämmerung • Fidelio • Norma • Carmen • Lucia di Lammermoor • Porgy and Bess • I Pagliacci • Cavalleria Rusticana • Le Nozze d
dermaus • Der Rosenkavalier • Rigoletto • Il Trovatore • La Traviata • Aida • Otello • Falstaff • Tristan und Isolde • Die Meistersinger von

GREAT
Opera
STORIES

GREAT

Opera
STORIES

THE PERFECT INTRODUCTION TO
THE MAGICAL WORLD OF OPERA

JEREMY HARWOOD

CHARTWELL
BOOKS, INC.

A QUINTET BOOK

Published by Chartwell Books
A Division of Book Sales, Inc.
110 Enterprise Avenue
Secaucus, New Jersey 07094

This edition produced for sale in the U.S.A., its
territories and dependencies only.

ISBN 1–55521–903–9

This book was designed and produced by
Quintet Publishing Limited
6 Blundell Street
London N7 9BH

Creative Director: Richard Dewing
Designer: Pete Laws
Project Editor: Stefanie Foster
Editor: Lydia Darbyshire

*Quintet Publishing would like to extend very special
thanks to Clive Thomas for contributing the*
Behind the Scenes *chapter*

Typeset in Great Britain by
Central Southern Typesetters, Eastbourne
Manufactured in Singapore by
Bright Arts Pte Limited
Printed in Hong Kong by
Leefung-Asco Printers Limited

CONTENTS

Introduction

When John Evelyn, the 17th-century British writer, visited Venice in 1645 he went to the opera and recorded the experience in his diary:

> *This night, having with my Lord Bruce taken our places before, we went to the Opera, where comedies and other plays are presented in recitative music, by the most excellent musicians, vocal and instrumental, with a variety of scenes painted and contrived with no less art of perspective, and machines for flying in the air, and other wonderful notions. Taken together, it is one of the most magnificent and expensive notions the wit of man can invent.*

Evelyn was obviously an instant opera convert, a person, who, in modern parlance, would be termed an opera buff. The world is full of them, and with the growth of televised opera this magical art form is reaching and appealing to a wider audience than ever before. Equally, though, opera has always aroused conflicting emotions and reactions. From Groucho Marx's laconic comment that "opera is never over until the fat lady sings" to fierce, determined attacks on it as costly and elitist, controversy has never been far away, inside and outside the opera house itself.

When the late Harold Rosenthal, the doyen of modern operatic critics, wrote his autobiography, he entitled it *My Mad, Mad World of Opera*. To the uninitiated, this is exactly what this world is. Who in their right minds, they argue, would be prepared to pay a small fortune or stand in line for hours to hear a lot of singers bawling away in languages that only a tiny percentage of the audience can understand? And what about the stories of the operas themselves? Aren't the majority of them improbable at best, and downright unbelievable at worst?

To this, there is no simple answer, or at least not one that will convince a critical diehard. What every opera-lover hopes for – and the stress is on "hope", for such expectations are, sadly, only rarely fulfilled – is that, on any given night, some magic spark will ignite – like Loge's flames in Wagner's *Ring* – and lift the performance, enabling it to take wing. It may come from the singers, the stage direction or the conductor, but, when it happens, the results are truly memorable. The hybrid, which is, after all what opera is, becomes a thoroughbred, with moving and unforgettable results. Here is one such moment: the author Robin May's description of the first

appearance of a young American mezzo-soprano on the stage of the Royal Opera House, Covent Garden, London, in the dress rehearsal of the 1963 revival of Verdi's *Don Carlos*:

The curtain rose on Visconti's beautiful setting and a few moments later, Grace Bumbry began to sing more thrillingly and beautifully than any mezzo that I have ever heard. She sang as wonderfully when I heard her at the second performance and, to judge by the notices, must have been sensational on the opening night. But that morning is the one I shall treasure – the memory of a dark-skinned beauty with gold in her throat.

Listen to any seasoned group of opera-goers in the bar or the theatre foyer during an interval, and the chances are that you will hear them swopping anecdotes and stories of some such performance when they themselves witnessed just such a miracle. These are the true opera buffs. For them, opera is an all-consuming passion, just as it was for Italians in the days of Verdi or, in 1830, for the Belgians, when a performance of a now almost forgotten opera, *La Muette de Portici* by the French composer Daniel Auber, sparked off the rising in Brussels that led to a national revolt against Dutch rule.

In the main, opera-lovers are discerning, although, if the voice is good enough, they will put up with a singer who looks completely wrong for a part and cannot act. Their real idols, however, are the great actor-singers – the Gobbis and Christoffs of yesterday and the Domingos and Behrens of today. As for composers, they recognize that Mozart, Verdi, Wagner and Puccini lie at the heart of the operatic repertory, but at the same time are on the look out for new experiences, which may range from the

revival of a long-forgotten Rossini *opera seria* to the première of a new work by a Tippett or a Glass. They recognize that stage direction has a vital role to play in opera production, although they may disagree with the results. On the whole, the days are long gone when a Patti could insist on having written into a contract a clause excusing her from rehearsal!

Opera in the 1990s is alive, well and healthy. Even Pierre Boulez, who, not so long ago, suggested that all the world's opera houses should be dynamited, has so changed his views as to appear on the podium in the orchestra pit. The Boulez/Chereau *Ring*, as recorded for posterity on disc and video at the Bayreuth Festival, is unquestionably one of the great operatic performances of our time, as is the Boulez/Stein *Peleas and Melisande* they conceived for Welsh National Opera. Their *Ring* also makes a perfect introduction to the dramatic possibilities of opera for the uninitiated.

But if you really want to hear an operatic genius at work and to understand what opera is about and how moving and inspiring it can be, turn to the recordings that Arturo Toscanini made of Verdi's *Otello* back in the 1940s, still available today. This is creation at white heat. Sometimes, notably in the concluding ensemble of Act 3, you can even hear the conductor singing along as he urges cast, chorus and orchestra to the ultimate effort.

What makes this recording unique is that it is a direct link with the past. The young Toscanini was actually a cello player in the orchestra of La Scala, Milan, for the opera's first performance. This is one of the great joys that opera-going can bring. Who knows – the performance you hear tonight may be the historic rendering of the work cited in the operatic histories of the day after tomorrow!

BEHIND THE SCENES

THE FIRST STAGES

Preparing a series of performances in a major opera house can be a lengthy process. The senior management, casting and technical departments are usually obliged to prepare provisional season plans about five years in advance. Factors such as the availability of star singers, an important conductor or a suitable producer inevitably influence early decisions by the opera season planners. An international opera will normally offer its public a repertoire of new productions each year, as well as a string of revivals, that is to say productions which have had a run of performances at least once and were successful enough to warrant being seen again.

REVIVALS

The "slotting in" of a revived opera is relatively easy compared with the complex process involved in mounting an entirely new production. The sets have already been constructed and stored, the costumes made, the chorus at the opera house will already have learnt the music and even the same solo singers may be engaged for the roles they sang previously. Furthermore, a revival is advantageous as technical problems will have already been encountered (and hopefully resolved), the lighting effects will have been carefully plotted and recorded on a computer disc and the management team will know how much rehearsal time will be required for the opera's restaging. The original producer will not usually be present to restage his own work – one of his assistants will be given this responsibility.

NEW PRODUCTIONS

An entirely new production, however, requires a very different organizational process, and, once the opera has been chosen, the management has many questions to consider. Who will be considered to produce it? Who is a suitable conductor for the style of music? Are these singers available to sing the major roles (not always so easy)? What budget can be afforded? Such questions must be

LEFT Music rehearsals and coaching often begin weeks before production rehearsals. The singers are guided by experienced pianists in matters of pronunciation, musical difficulties and interpretation of the role.

asked in the very early stages of planning, and always with the need for a critical success in mind.

Once a producer has accepted the invitation to work on a new production, and his availability has been confirmed, he must prepare one or more collaborators to create sets and costumes for him, and later, the lighting for the show. The sets must be designed with accurate drawings, plans and models, budgeted and examined by the technical director of the opera house, and suitable companies considered for building sets, handling properties and making costumes which cannot be done by company personnel. The producer and his designer decide together what the style, period and function of the sets should be, and when designs and models are presented to the management and the technical director for approval, the first ideas are often rejected, for various reasons: the scenery may cost too much to build, it may not fit in the theatre easily, entail too many changes, be too difficult to light successfully or be acoustically unsatisfactory for the singers.

Eventually, however, the right design will be accepted and a senior figure in the technical department, the production manager, can set to work on the project, organizing and co-ordinating the construction process in close consultation with the opera's designer.

SETS

The construction of the sets, often a different design for each scene or act of the opera, will begin several months before they are due to appear on stage for rehearsals. Again, budgetary and technical problems will continue to arise. Certain materials will be too expensive, unsuitable or simply unavailable. Consequently, a designer will rarely be easily pleased. After all, from a series of sketches, plans and matchstick reproductions, full-size, three-dimensional working scenery has to appear, often with several moving components, and electronic or hydraulic devices integral to the design.

COSTUMES

As for the costumes, these may or may not be created by the designer of the sets. A large team of skilled tailors, seamstresses, costume buyers and wardrobe managers are par for the course in every opera house. Once approved, the long realization

ABOVE Decoration of sets often occurs on a massive scale, and the final props can turn out quite differently from what was originally envisaged.

process of the costume designs begins, a process somewhat different from the exactness expected of set designs. Much freedom is necessarily afforded to wardrobe staff in interpreting the designer's ideas, since a sketch, no matter how precise, needs to be transformed into a pattern and finally the costume itself to fit the chosen singer for the role. Fabrics need to be chosen, purchased, cut and dyed, often in vast quantities since the entire chorus has to be clothed as well as the soloists, actors and dancers in the show. This could mean 400 costumes in a classic grand opera such as *Turandot* or *Aida*. Remember, also, that these all need to be individually fitted on each and every member of the cast. There will always be a team of wig and makeup specialists working at the costume designer's side, and if the work necessitates a period flavour, hours of meticulous work will be undertaken to create authentic wigs which must complement the costumes.

THE MUSIC

Let us return to the planning offices in the opera house. While the production team is being finalized, the casting director will be busy searching for singers, usually through established agencies or auditions. Many months, or even years in some cases, will be involved in negotiating with agents in order to engage specific singers for precise rehearsal and performance periods. The earlier this is done the better because busy and established singers inevitably have dates when they are already booked for other engagements, often in different cities or countries.

The conductor and producer will probably have to put up with these absences during the rehearsal periods. Indeed, the singer may have even been contracted before them. However, many producers now insist on realistic rehearsal time as well as a credible physique, age and stage manner for their productions. Often serious compromises are made, therefore, when trying to cast a suitable timbre of voice with the right appearance.

A singer is usually contractually obliged to arrive for his or her first production rehearsal knowing the given role by heart. Often a singer is engaged, however, primarily for his or her previous success in the role elsewhere, and will already possess a thorough dramatic and musical understanding of it. Once a cast for an opera has been established, music rehearsals and coaching

may begin, sometimes several weeks before the production rehearsals. These coaching sessions are given by experienced pianists who help singers with problems of foreign language pronunciation, interpretation of the role or simply difficulties with the music itself. Of course, the singer may have his or her own teachers and coaches and may prefer to work independently.

As for the conductor, he may or may not have a say in the casting depending on his importance or insistence, and he will probably not meet the singers and producer before the first day of staging rehearsals. The relationship between the conductor and producer is of paramount importance – a good rapport and mutual consideration being essential for a truly cohesive result. After all, what is the most important aspect of opera, the drama or the music?

REHEARSALS

After months of diligent preparation and coordination, rehearsals finally begin. This is a time of little rest for all concerned. Singers, actors, dancers, rehearsal pianists, producer and conductor all come together for the first time in the rehearsal hall, with the stage marked out on the floor and substitutes for real props and costumes at the ready. The stage manager and his team arrive on the scene and from this moment on the stage manager is the primary coordinator for the production, liaising between the artists, producer, conductor, production manager, technical staff and opera house management for every sort of difficulty, concern or unforeseen circumstance.

Example of the production schedule for an opera

3-5 YEARS
- Management chooses opera.
- Star singers engaged.
- Producer and conductor considered.
- Provisional performance dates planned.

1-2 YEARS
- Producer chooses designers.
- Budget of opera decided.
- Designs accepted.
- Casting continues.
- Performance dates decided.

6 MONTHS-1 YEAR
- Chorus learn music.
- Sets and costumes begin construction.
- Casting completed for soloists.
- Rehearsal schedules drafted.

2-6 MONTHS
- Planning schedules completed.
- Music coaching begins.
- Sets and costumes continue construction.
- Casting of actors, dancers and understudies.

6-8 WEEKS
- Rehearsals begin with piano.
- Orchestra rehearse alone.
- Costume fittings begin.

The stage management team is responsible for carefully documenting the production from beginning to end with stage movements, entrances, changes of scenery and other technical effects such as lighting and sound. The stage management are also there to ensure that singers know whenever they are required.

Rehearsals on the stage in the opera house itself will take place probably three or four weeks later. The singers will still rehearse with the piano initially, so that the producer can still change subtleties of staging and technical problems can be overcome. During the final days, however, the orchestra will join the stage rehearsals having already been rehearsed separately by the conductor. At this stage, the director must have completed his staging, and must sit back and let the conductor control the pace of the rehearsals. The final days are also vital for the technical staff of the opera house, this precious time being spent regulating the lighting, perfecting the scene changes and adding the finishing touches to the sets.

Fortunately for all concerned, there are usually complete runs of the opera on stage before the opening night, in order to familiarize artists and technicians alike with realistic performance conditions. The very final rehearsal – the "general" or "dress rehearsal" – is often open to an invited audience and it is the true test for all those who have been involved.

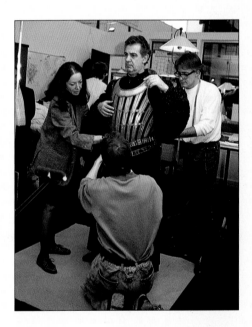

LEFT Singers are carefully directed by the stage director in their acting roles – their theatrical performances are of as great importance as their singing. Here Roman Polanski provides inspiration by his example.

RIGHT Costume design and production can be a lengthy process, as every single singer has to be fitted, and his or her physique and bearing taken into account. Accordingly, the wardrobe staff are allowed a certain flexibility when interpreting original sketches. Here Placido Domingo is being fitted for his role in *Otello*.

– 3 WEEKS
Rehearsals in theatre with piano.
Non-stop technical work on sets and lights.
Singers join with orchestra for first time.

1 – 2 WEEKS
● Stage rehearsals with orchestra.
● Lighting begins to be plotted.
● Final changes to sets and costumes.

2 – 3 DAYS
● Final dress rehearsal.

LUDWIG VAN

Beethoven (1770–1827)

FIDELIO

Opera in two acts, libretto by Joseph Sonnleithner and Georg Friedrich Treitschke after the play by Jean Nicholas Bouilly.

One of the greatest composers of all time, Ludwig van Beethoven settled in Vienna in 1792 after studying there with Haydn. At the age of 30, he started to go deaf, but this did not stop him composing a stream of master-works, including the greatest of his nine symphonies, his revolutionary late string quartets and his towering** Missa Solemnis. **Often boorish, temperamental and lonely, his last years were clouded by further illness.

F*IDELIO. oder die Eheliche Liebe (Fidelio,* or *Married Love)* was first performed at the Theater an der Wien, Vienna, on 20 November 1805 in its original three-act version. It was revised and revived in two acts on 29 March 1806; the final version, as performed today, received its première in Vienna in 1814. The first performance in Britain was at the Haymarket Theatre, London, in 1832; the first performance in the USA took place in New York in 1839.

Fidelio is Beethoven's only opera. After Mozart's *Die Zauberflöte (The Magic Flute)*, it was the second great German opera to be composed and, like its magical predecessor, it was cast in the form of a *singspiel* – that is, a work combining music with spoken dialogue, as opposed to the sung recitatives of formal grand opera. However, unlike *Die Zauberflöte, Fidelio* (then titled *Leonora*) was a failure at its first performance. There were several reasons for this, one being that Vienna was occupied at the time by the French, and much of the audience consisted of soldiers of Napoleon's victorious army. Beethoven himself was quick to realize, however, that the work was flawed, and a third revised version triumphed on its first performance in 1814. Today, *Fidelio* is a cornerstone of the repertory of every great opera house throughout the world.

Although Beethoven never returned to the opera house, the pains he took over his sole opera are evident on every page of the score. Indeed, he wrote no fewer than four overtures for the work – *Leonora 1, 2* and *3* as well as the *Fidelio* overture itself. Beethoven, it is thought, recognized that the weight and drama of his first thoughts were inappropriate for the domestic nature of the opening scene; the practice of interpolating *Leonora No. 3* before the final scene of the opera dates from the mid-19th century.

CAST

Marcellina
Rocco's daughter
Soprano

Jacquino
the prison doorkeeper
Tenor

Rocco
chief jailer
Bass

Leonora
wife of Florestan, disguised as Fidelio
Soprano

Don Pizarro
governor of the prison
Baritone

Florestan
a Spanish nobleman
Tenor

Don Fernando
the king's minister
Baritone

Chorus
Soldiers, prisoners and people

RIGHT **The prisoners make their way across the courtyard of the fortress, marvelling at the unaccustomed sunlight. In the absence of Don Pizarro, Leonora, disguised as Fidelio, has persuaded Rocco to allow them out of their cells in honour of the king's birthday.**

ACT ONE

SCENE 1

Don Pizarro, the rascally governor of a Spanish prison, has wrongly imprisoned his enemy, Don Florestan. Leonora, Florestan's loyal wife, has disguised herself as a young man, Fidelio, and, in order to search for him, has taken employment in the prison as the assistant to Rocco, the head gaoler. The curtain rises on a domestic scene: Marcellina, Rocco's daughter, is discovered doing her ironing. Jacquino, the gatekeeper and Marcellina's former sweetheart, enters to woo her, but she manages to avoid the issue. After Jacquino leaves in frustration, she tells us that she has fallen in love with the gentle Fidelio. Rocco then enters, to be followed by Leonora in her male disguise. The gaoler is also greatly taken with Fidelio and remarks on the fancy he believes and hopes the two young people have taken for each other, an episode that leads up to the great quartet "Mir ist so wunderbar" ("How wonderful, this emotion"), in which the three are joined by Jacquino, who has returned to the scene. Rocco urges Fidelio to press his suit, telling him that all he needs to succeed in life is money. He then describes the state of the prisoners, including that of one who is held in solitary con-

finement in the deepest dungeon of the fortress. Fidelio seizes on the revelation – can this be the husband she has come to save? The three sum up their conflicting emotions in a final trio.

ACT ONE

SCENE 2

A short orchestral march heralds the approach of Pizarro. He opens a letter to find a warning from a friend in Madrid that Don Fernando, an old friend of Florestan, is about to inspect the fortress as Minister of State. Pizarro, realizing that he faces ruin if Florestan is discovered, decides to have him murdered. He posts a sentry on the battlements, ordering him to trumpet a signal as soon as the ministerial procession comes into sight, and then bribes Rocco to help him in his murderous scheme, although the latter refuses to do more than prepare a grave. Their plotting has been overheard by Fidelio, who gives vent to her emotions in the magnificent aria "Abscheulicher! Wo eilst du hin?" ("Villain! Whither are you hastening?") Rocco re-enters and tells Fidelio to prepare to help him to dig the grave.

It is the king's birthday and a sunny day. Taking advantage of Rocco's benevolence and the tem-

Fidelio

RIGHT At the climax of the dungeon scene Leonora throws herself between the villainous Pizarro and her husband, Florestan, with the cry "Töt 'erst sein Weib!" ("First kill his wife!").

porary absence of Pizarro, Fidelio pleads with him to allow the prisoners out of their cells, if only for a short time. One by one, they emerge, their chorus swelling up to a mighty hymn and then subsiding again. Pizarro angrily returns to order the prisoners back to their cells, and, as they bid farewell to their brief period of freedom, the act comes to an end.

ACT TWO After an orchestral prelude, we find
SCENE 1 ourselves in Florestan's cell, where he is confined in heavy chains. He sings of his lost liberty and his faith that, even now, an "angel" is working for his deliverance. As he faints, Rocco and Fidelio enter and start their gruesome task of digging the grave. Florestan appeals to them for a crust of bread and a drink of water; as Fidelio tends to his needs, she recognizes her husband.

Pizarro enters, dagger poised, for his vengeance. A dramatic quartet follows, culminating with Fidelio holding a pistol to Pizarro's head, telling him that, before despatching Florestan, he will kill Leonora. At that moment the trumpet sounds. Don Fernando has arrived and Pizarro hurries off to meet him, followed by Rocco. Florestan and Leonora celebrate their deliverance in the duet "O, namenlose Freude" ("Oh, inexpressible joy").

ACT TWO The garrison prisoners and people
SCENE 2 muster to greet the minister. Leonora leads in Florestan, whom Don Fernando immediately recognizes as the friend he thought dead. Rocco reveals Pizarro's plot and his arrest follows. Leonora frees Florestan from his chains, Marcellina is reunited with Jacquino and a chorus of general rejoicing brings the opera to an end.

VINCENZO *Bellini* (1801–35)

NORMA

Opera in two acts, libretto by Felice Romani, based on a tragedy by Soumet

CAST

Oroveso
arch-Druid of the
Gauls, Norma's
father
Bass

Pollione
Roman pro-consul
Tenor

Flavio
a centurion
Tenor

Norma
high priestess of the
Druids
Soprano

Adalgisa
a temple virgin
Mezzo-soprano

Clotilda
Norma's confidant
Soprano

Chorus
Druids, priestesses,
Gallic warriors

NORMA was first performed at La Scala, Milan, on 26 December 1831. The first performance in Britain was at the Haymarket Theatre, London, in 1833; the first performance in the USA took place in New Orleans in 1836.

With his Italian contemporary (and arch-rival) Donizetti, Bellini is a master of what is known as the *bel canto* style, although when it is performed by lesser artists the term has sometimes been disparagingly adapted to *can belto!* Whether as a result of this or of changing fashions or a combination of both factors, *Norma*, in common with Bellini's other operas, practically vanished from the repertory for many decades. Its re-emergence in recent years was due largely to the appearance of sopranos such as Maria Callas, Dame Joan Sutherland and Montserrat Caballe, who could do full justice to what is universally regarded as one of the most demanding of operatic parts, both vocally and dramatically.

Vincenzo Bellini died young, before he could reach his full brilliance. During his short life, he wrote 11 operas, of which Norma, La Sonnambula (The Sleepwalker) and I Puritani (The Puritans) are the ones most frequently revived today. Bellini was a master of the art of writing long, flowing vocal lines; all his works, however, demand outstanding singers to do justice to their melodically beautiful vocal parts.

ACT ONE

SCENE 1

In the sacred grove of the Druids, Oroveso, accompanied by his followers, is praying to the gods to rally the people and help bring about the overthrow of the hated Roman conquerors. No sooner have they left the grove than two Romans, Pollione, the pro-consul, and his friend, Flavio, enter. Pollione tells Flavio that although he had once loved Norma – indeed, she is the mother of his two children – his heart is now given to the young priestess Adalgisa. Interrupted by the sound of the returning Druids, the two men flee.

A dramatic march heralds the approach of the Druid priests and priestesses, Norma at their head. In the aria "Casta Diva" ("Chaste goddess") she reveals her mixed emotions. Seeking to protect her faithless lover, she counsels the Gauls that the

release Adalgisa from her vows when Pollione enters and she realizes that he is the Roman whom Adalgisa loves. In an exciting trio, the three give vent to their emotions, Pollione still begging Adalgisa to fly with him, while she turns away from him in horror as the betrayer of her high priestess.

ACT TWO

SCENE 1 The scene is as before. Filled with despair, Norma is standing over her children's cradle. She agonizes over whether to kill them and then herself, but resolves instead to renounce her love. She summons Adalgisa and begs her to marry Pollione and to take her place as the children's mother. But in the duet "Mira, O Norma" ("See, oh Norma") Adalgisa protests that, although she will meet Pollione one last time, it will be only to remind him of his duty to Norma.

ACT TWO

SCENE 2 Back in the sacred grove, Oroveso again calls for action, but Norma temporizes until Adalgisa returns with the news that Pollione is deaf even to her entreaties. Norma's emotions are beyond control. She strikes the great war gong, summons the Druids and leads them in a determined chorus, calling for war. A noise is heard in the temple, whose guards rush off and drag in the intruder. It is Pollione, who has made a last attempt to carry off Adalgisa.

Norma orders the Druids to leave her alone with the prisoner and confronts Pollione for the last time. To save him from death, she calls the Druids back and makes the ultimate sacrifice, revealing how she has betrayed her own sacred vows. Having consigned her children to Oroveso's care, she mounts the pyre that had been prepared for Pollione. But she is not alone. Pollione, his love for Norma rekindled, joins her. As the flames rise, the two sing of their love, while Oroveso and the chorus bemoan Norma's fate. The curtain falls.

time is not yet ripe for them to rise against the Roman oppressors. Rome, she says, will fall through its own weakness, rather than through any deeds of theirs. At the same time, she prays to the goddess to help her recapture Pollione's love.

The Druids disperse, and Adalgisa enters the deserted grove to await Pollione. In a dramatic duet, Pollione begs her to fly with him to the safety of Rome, and, after some hesitation, she agrees to his plan.

ACT ONE

SCENE 2 Inside her hut Norma bemoans her lot. She realizes that Pollione plans to desert her and their children for a new love, but she does not know her rival's name. At that moment, Adalgisa enters to seek Norma's counsel. She confesses she has betrayed her temple vows by falling in love – and with a Roman. Norma, mindful of her own predicament, is sympathetic, and she is about to

GEORGES *B izet* (1838–75)

CARMEN

Opera in three acts, libretto by Henri Meilhac and Ludovic Halévy, after the novel by Prosper Merimée

CAST

Morales
a sergeant
Baritone

Micaela
a peasant girl
Soprano

Don José
a corporal of
dragoons
Tenor

Zuniga
his lieutenant
Bass

Carmen
a gypsy
Soprano

Frasquita
a gypsy
Soprano

Mercedes
a gypsy
Soprano

Escamillo
a toreador
Baritone

Dancairo
a smuggler
Tenor

Remendado
a smuggler
Baritone

Innkeeper, guide,
officers, soldiers,
boys, cigarette girls,
gypsies, smugglers,
citizens

ARMEN was first performed at the Opéra-Comique, Paris, on 3 March 1875. It was first played in Britain (in Italian) at Her Majesty's Theatre, London, on 22 January 1878; the first performance in the USA was at the Academy of Music, New York, on 23 October 1879.

Carmen is unquestionably one of the world's most popular operas, yet not only was its first performance a fiasco, but, until relatively recently, it was universally performed in a version far from what Bizet intended. He conceived the piece as an *opéra comique* (despite its tragic story and ending), in which a substantial part of the action was carried out in spoken dialogue. The recitatives with which we are familiar today were created for a revival in Vienna and were not written by Bizet at all, but by his pupil and colleague Ernest Guiraud. It was this version that took the world's opera stages by storm, but, by this time, the exhausted, disenchanted composer was already dead.

When we listen to this brilliant, gripping score, the reason for *Carmen*'s initial failure is a mystery. At the time, however, the orchestra and chorus of the Opéra-Comique complained that some of the music was unplayable and unsingable. More importantly, the spicy realism of the story was frowned on by the audience of one of the most respectable theatres of the day. What Bizet offered – working-class girls smoking on stage, for instance – proved totally unpalatable, despite its Spanish setting, to the bourgeois Parisians of 1875.

ACT ONE After an orchestral prelude, the curtain rises on a square in Seville, dominated by a cigarette factory and a guard post, in front of which Morales and his fellow soldiers are lounging, watching the passers-by. A young, shy, country girl, Micaela, enters in search of her fiancé, Don José, but, learning that he will not arrive until the

Having studied under Gounod and Halevy, the young Georges Bizet won the prestigious Prix de Rome in 1857. However, his career was dogged by lack of success; the symphony he wrote in 1855 – even before he won his prize – remained undiscovered until 1935, while the virulent attacks launched by critics and public alike on Carmen undoubtedly hastened his untimely death.

ARMEN was first performed at the Opéra-Comique, Paris, on 3 March 1875. It was first played in Britain (in Italian) at Her Majesty's Theatre, London, on 22 January 1878; the first performance in the USA was at the Academy of Music, New York, on 23 October 1879.

Carmen is unquestionably one of the world's most popular operas, yet not only was its first performance a fiasco, but, until relatively recently, it was universally performed in a version far from what Bizet intended. He conceived the piece as an *opéra comique* (despite its tragic story and ending), in which a substantial part of the action was carried out in spoken dialogue. The recitatives with which we are familiar today were created for a revival in Vienna and were not written by Bizet at all, but by his pupil and colleague Ernest Guiraud. It was this version that took the world's opera stages by storm, but, by this time, the exhausted, disenchanted composer was already dead.

When we listen to this brilliant, gripping score, the reason for *Carmen*'s initial failure is a mystery. At the time, however, the orchestra and chorus of the Opéra-Comique complained that some of the music was unplayable and unsingable. More importantly, the spicy realism of the story was frowned on by the audience of one of the most respectable theatres of the day. What Bizet offered – working-class girls smoking on stage, for instance – proved totally unpalatable, despite its Spanish setting, to the bourgeois Parisians of 1875.

ACT ONE After an orchestral prelude, the curtain rises on a square in Seville, dominated by a cigarette factory and a guard post, in front of which Morales and his fellow soldiers are lounging, watching the passers-by. A young, shy, country girl, Micaela, enters in search of her fiancé, Don José, but, learning that he will not arrive until the

Carmen

changing of the guard and put off by the soldiers' attempts to flirt with her, she runs off, promising to return. A distant bugle call sounds, followed by another, and the orchestra strikes up a march. Preceded by a band of urchins imitating their step, the relief guard enters, headed by Zuniga and José. Morales tells José that a young woman has been looking for him, and he recognizes Micaela from the description.

Zuniga asks José what the large building is, and he explains that it is a cigarette factory. Zuniga is keen to see the girls who roll the cigarettes; as the factory bell signals the start of work, he joins the crowd gathering in the square. The cigarette girls enter, but it is soon noticed that one of their number is missing – Carmencita (Carmen). Suddenly she enters, to be surrounded by a group of admirers pledging their love. In reply, she sings the celebrated *habañera* "L'amour est un oiseau rebelle" (Love is like a wild bird"), warning anyone who loves her to beware.

Carmen directs the second verse of her song at the handsome José, but he steadfastly ignores her,

LEFT **Carmen warns her galaxy of admirers that while she may be passionate, she is fickle. Any man who loves her, she sings, had best beware.**

BELOW **The smugglers try to persuade Carmen and her friends to help them in their latest escapade. Carmen refuses. The smugglers suggest that she persuades her lover to join their band.**

even when she tosses a flower at him before running off laughing with her workmates. As the crowd disperses, José quickly stoops down to pick up the discarded flower and hides it in his tunic. Micaela returns, bringing José news from home in the duet "Parle-moi de ma mère" ("Tell me the news of my mother"). In the letter Micaela hands José, which he reads aloud, his mother urges him to marry his sweetheart and the confused girl runs off, saying she will return for his reply.

José's thoughts are interrupted by cries of alarm from the factory, and the cigarette girls run out, calling for help. Carmen has quarrelled with and stabbed a girl. Zuniga orders José and two other dragoons into the factory to bring the gypsy before him. When Zuniga questions her, however, she refuses to reply and the exasperated lieutenant orders José to tie her up and guard her, while he writes the warrant for her arrest.

Alone with José, Carmen's fatal charm begins to cast its spell and the bewitched dragoon unties her hands, leaving the rope around her wrists as though she were still captive. Zuniga re-enters,

but, as the chorus returns, she pushes the soldiers aside and escapes. As the crowd mocks the discomforted Zuniga, he orders José's arrest.

ACT TWO In Lillas Pastia's tavern near to the city walls some gypsy girls are dancing, and Carmen, together with her friends Mercedes and Frasquita, join in the wild dance. Zuniga and his fellow officers try to persuade them to go with them to the theatre, but they refuse. Zuniga tells Carmen that José, who was sentenced to a month in prison for having connived at her escape, has just been released, but she affects unconcern.

An off-stage chorus is heard, saluting the toreador Escamillo, and Zuniga invites him in to drink his health. Escamillo's reply takes the form of a series of couplets, describing his feelings in the bull ring. Struck by Carmen's attraction, he whispers he will dedicate the next bull he kills to her, but she tells him to put all thoughts of her out of his mind – for the moment. She also warns Zuniga not to return.

19

LEFT Carmen scornfully accuses Don José of having never cared for her. In reply, he passionately declares his love. He has even kept the flower she threw to him when they first met.

RIGHT As José becomes more and more importunate and jealous, Carmen turns against him, living up to her earlier warning to her admirers to beware of her. The dashing toreador Escamillo is her new love.

OPPOSITE As the crowd begins to leave the bull-ring, Don José confesses that, maddened by jealousy and Carmen's desertion, he has stabbed his beloved to death.

The tavern clears and Carmen and her two friends are left alone with the innkeeper, Lillas Pastia. The smugglers Dancairo and Remendado enter to talk over business with the three girls. They need their help to transport their smuggled contraband, but this time Carmen refuses to throw in her lot with theirs. She is, she declares, in love with José and, as they bet he will not dare return to her, he is heard singing off-stage. As they leave, the smugglers tell Carmen she should persuade José to join them.

José enters, and Carmen arouses his passions by telling him of her dance. Now, she will dance for him alone, but no sooner has she started than a trumpet is heard, sounding the retreat. As José prepares to leave, Carmen angrily accuses him of not loving her. In reply, he sings movingly of his devotion in "La fleur que tu m'avais jetée" ("The flower that once you threw to me"), but she is not placated, trying to persuade him to desert and run away with her. Instead, he rushes towards the door, attempting to say goodbye to her for ever.

There is a knock and José is halted in his tracks. It is Zuniga, who orders him back to barracks. The two men prepare to fight, and Carmen calls the smugglers to her aid. Zuniga is led away and José has no alternative but to join the smugglers.

ACT THREE
SCENE 1
High in the mountains. It is night. A smuggler enters, gives a signal and the rest of the band enters, including José, who is ill-at-ease. Carmen is tiring of him already, and he is torn by thoughts of his mother who lives nearby. Carmen exclaims that he can leave for all she cares, but he warns that she will never survive their separation. Leaving him to brood, she joins her friends, who are telling their fortunes by cards. When Carmen takes her turn, however, she repeatedly turns up the ace of spades, the card of death.

The girls are sent off to distract the customs men, the smugglers following. José is left behind on guard. Unseen by him, a guide leads Micaela onto the scene. She has come to reclaim José, but

suddenly she sees him fire his rifle at some unseen target. The terrified girl swiftly conceals herself behind some rocks. José's target was Escamillo, who, having heard that her latest love affair is over, has come in search of Carmen. José draws his dagger and the two men fight. Escamillo slips and José is at his throat, only for Escamillo to be rescued by Carmen, who throws herself between them. Escamillo leaves, inviting the smugglers to his next bull-fight, but, as they prepare to follow, Micaela is dragged in. José rejects her appeals to leave the smugglers, especially when Carmen joins in, but when she tells him that his mother is dying, he consents to go with her. He warns Carmen, however, that she has not seen the last of him and that they will meet again. As Escamillo is heard singing off-stage, the curtain falls.

ACT THREE
SCENE 2 The square before the bull-ring in Seville, on the day of the great bull-fight, is a hive of activity, with street-sellers plying their wares to the gather-ing crowd. The ceremonial procession of bull-fighters makes its way through the throng, culmin-ating with the entrance of Escamillo, Carmen on his arm. He enters the arena, but, as Carmen makes to follow, she is accosted by Frasquita and Mercedes. They warn her that José is in the crowd, but, rather than escape, as they advise, she defiantly stays to face him.

The former lovers are alone – "C'est toi!" (So it's you!"). José makes a final appeal to Carmen to return to him, but, as she hears the crowd hailing Escamillo's victory, she makes to sweep past him. As he grapples with her, she declares her love for Escamillo, and the maddened José draws his knife. She hurls the ring he once gave her in his face, and he stabs her to the heart. She falls dead as a renewed chorus of victory breaks out off-stage.

José stands like a man in a trance. As some passers-by re-enter, he sobs "Vous pouvez m'arrêter . . . c'est moi qui l'ai tuée . . . ma Carmen adorée" ("You can arrest me . . . I killed her . . . my beloved Carmen"). The curtain falls.

Donizetti (1797–1848)

LUCIA DI LAMMERMOOR

Opera in three acts, libretto by Salvatore Cammarano after the novel The Bride of Lammermoor *by Sir Walter Scott*

Gaetano Donizetti outlived his great rival Bellini, but became paralyzed and mentally ill towards the end of his life. Of his 75 stage works, the best known, in addition to Lucia di Lammermoor, is the historical opera Maria Stuarda – though its romantic view of Tudor history is far from reality – and the brilliant comic opera Don Pasquale.

Lucia *di Lammermoor* was first performed at the Teatro San Carlo, Naples, on 26 September 1835. It was first heard in Britain at Her Majesty's Theatre, London, in April 1838; the first American performance took place at New Orleans in 1841.

Together with his comic opera *Don Pasquale*, *Lucia di Lammermoor* is generally held to be Donizetti's finest work. This, however, did not save it from a long period of neglect, when it was dismissed as the canary fanciers' opera *par excellence*. Its revival was sparked off by the emergence of Maria Callas as the Lucia of her day; the same acclaim was accorded to Dame Joan Sutherland in her long dominance of the role, which began with her first appearance as Lucia at the Royal Opera House, Covent Garden, London, in 1959.

ACT ONE
SCENE 1
A wood, near Lammermoor Castle. Normanno tells Enrico that he suspects that Lucia and Edgardo have been meeting secretly in the castle park. Normanno has accordingly sent his huntsmen to confirm or disprove his suspicions. Enrico is furious. Not only, unknown to Lucia, is he plotting her marriage to Lord Arturo Bucklaw to rescue his failing fortunes, but the Ashtons and the Ravenswoods have for long been locked in a deadly feud. When the huntsmen confirm that Normanno is correct, Enrico swears vengeance.

ACT ONE
SCENE 2
The park, near a fountain. Lucia appears with her companion Alisa, to whom she relates the sad legend of thwarted love associated with the place in the aria "Regnava nel silenzio" ("All was silent"). But she throws off her sad mood in anticipation of seeing Edgardo again – "Quando rapita" ("Swift

ABOVE Lucia has murdered her husband on their wedding night. Driven insane by grief and remorse, she imagines that she is reunited with Edgardo in a coloratura *tour de force* that is the greatest *bel canto* mad scene ever composed.

forged by himself, in which Edgardo admits to betraying her. Although believing herself deserted, Lucia is still reluctant to fall in with Enrico's plan until she hears that only by consenting to the marriage can she save her brother from a traitor's death, a plea reinforced by Raymondo, the castle chaplain.

ACT TWO SCENE 2 The guests assemble in the great hall of the castle to witness the signing of the marriage contract. After an exchange of courtesies between Enrico and Arturo, Lucia enters. Arturo comments on her sadness, but Enrico explains this away by saying that she is still mourning her recently deceased mother. Lucia and Arturo sign the contract, at which moment the dour figure of Edgardo stalks into the banqueting hall. The sextet that follows, "Chi mi frena il tal momento?" ("What holds me back at this moment?"), is, when properly sung, one of the greatest of all ensembles in 19th-century Italian opera. Edgardo rounds on Lucia for her treachery and, as she collapses, with the guests swearing vengeance on him, the curtain falls.

ACT THREE SCENE 1 This scene in Edgardo's castle, in which Enrico arrives to challenge him to a duel, is usually cut in modern performance.

ACT THREE SCENE 2 The wedding guests are still feasting, but their revels are interrupted by a horror-struck Raymondo. Lucia has gone mad and killed her luckless husband. The deranged heroine now appears. The "mad scene" that follows is divided into two sections – a slow, dream-like opening, in which Lucia imagines that she has been reunited with, and married to, Edgardo, and a final *cabaletta*, which is the ultimate test of vocal virtuosity, as the soprano trills and sings in company with a solo flute.

ACT THREE SCENE 3 A churchyard, where Edgardo's ancestors lie buried. Edgardo is bemoaning his fate when the sound of a funeral procession is heard, and Raymondo brings him the news of Lucia's madness and subsequent death. There is nothing left for him to live for and he kills himself as the curtain falls.

as thought"). Edgardo duly enters, but only to bid Lucia farewell. In a duet, he tells her he has been ordered to France by the king, but that he will return to claim her as his wife. They vow eternal love.

ACT TWO SCENE 1 A room in the castle. Lucia protests to Enrico about the marriage into which he is trying to force her, but now her brother plays his trump card. He shows her a letter, supposedly from Edgardo but really

GEORGE *Gershwin* (1898–1937)

PORGY AND BESS

Opera in three acts, libretto by du Bose and Dorothy Heyward and Ira Gershwin

With his brother Ira, who wrote many of the lyrics for his songs, George Gershwin wrote dozens of Broadway hits, including **The Man I Love, I Got Rhythm** and **Lady Be Good.** *He saw* **Porgy and Bess,** *along with his orchestral works* **Rhapsody in Blue, An American in Paris** *and* **Piano Concert,** *as bridging the gap between popular and classical music, hoping to attract a new audience to opera house and concert hall.*

PORGY *and Bess* was first performed in Boston on 30 September 1935; it reached Britain in autumn 1953 as part of an all-black company's European tour. Notable revivals have included one at the Metropolitan Opera, New York, in 1985, the Glyndebourne Festival production of the following year and the Royal Opera House, Covent Garden, adaptation of the Glyndebourne staging in 1992.

Porgy and Bess was the first American opera to become a substantial worldwide success. Written in jazz idiom, it has survived, while other jazz operas, such as Ernest Křenek's 1927 *Jonny spielt auf (Johnny Plays On)* have largely vanished from the stage. The terms of Gershwin's will prohibit its production in English-speaking countries with non-black casts; paradoxically, productions sung in translation may employ white singers in the appropriate make-up.

ACT ONE
SCENE 1
We are inside Catfish Row, a black tenement on the waterfront of Charleston, South Carolina, and are being introduced to the night life of the building. Above the general singing and dancing, a lazy, seductive lullaby, sung by Clara as she nurses her baby, slowly rises. This is "Summertime", one of the best known songs in the score. The stage lights fade, only to brighten again to focus on another part of the stage, where a crap game is going on. Jake, Clara's husband, offers to send the child to sleep; he sings "A woman is a sometime thing", but a howl from the baby ends the episode.

Peter the honey man's call heralds the arrival of the crippled Porgy. The crowd teases him about his love life. Jake opines that Porgy is "soft on Crown's Bess", but Porgy defends her against such slanders. He laments his lonely, crippled state, only to be interrupted by the entrance of Crown,

CAST

Clara Jake's wife *Soprano*	**Robbins** a neighbour *Tenor*	**Mr Archdale** a white man *Spoken*
Jake a fisherman *Baritone*	**Sportin' Life** a drugs pedlar *Tenor*	**Lily** Peter's wife *Mezzo-soprano*
Peter the honey man *Tenor*	**Serena** Robbins's wife *Soprano*	**Jim** a cotton picker *Baritone*
Porgy a cripple *Baritone-bass*	**Undertaker** *Baritone*	**Chorus** Detective, policeman, Coroner, Scipio (a small boy), inhabitants of Catfish Row
Crown a stevedore *Bass*	**Maria** keeper of the cookshop *Contralto*	
Bess Crown's girl *Soprano*	**Frazier** a "lawyer" *Baritone*	

who is drunk, and Bess. Crown joins the crap players, loses heavily to Robbins and turns on him with a cotton hook, killing him in the subsequent brawl. Bess gives Crown money and urges him to flee; Sportin' Life offers to take Bess to New York, but she rebuffs him. As police whistles blow, she tries to find shelter in Catfish Row until Porgy takes pity on her and lets her into his room.

ACT ONE In Serena's room. Robbins's body is laid out on the bed, a saucer on
SCENE 2 his chest for funeral contributions. Porgy and Bess are among the mourners and Porgy leads them in a spiritual. A detective enters and accuses Peter of the murder. Although the others now incriminate Crown, Peter is still taken off as a "material witness". Porgy reflects on this injustice, while Serena sings a lament for her dead husband. The undertaker eventually agrees to bury him for the few dollars in the saucer, and the scene concludes with another spiritual, "Oh, we're leaving for the Promise' Land".

ABOVE "Summertime and the goin' is easy" – this lazy lullaby is one of the greatest moments in Gershwin's magical score. Life in the tenement at Catfish Row is played out before our eyes in this intensely theatrical scene.

ACT TWO

SCENE 1 A month later. Jake and his fellow fishermen are repairing their nets. Porgy appears at his window, singing a catchy banjo song, and they comment on how much happier he seems now he is living with Bess. Maria, the cook, turns on Sportin' Life for peddling drugs, only desisting when Frazier arrives to "sell" Porgy a divorce for Bess, explaining that it is far more expensive to divorce someone who is not married. He is followed by a white visitor, Mr Archdale, who tells Porgy he will stand bail for Peter. Porgy catches sight of a buzzard, a bird of ill omen, and then, having caught Sportin' Life offering drugs to Bess, warns him to keep away.

The rest of the company prepare to leave for a picnic, but Bess tells Porgy that she will stay with him. The two sing an extended love duet, "Bess, you is my woman now", at the end of which the picnickers depart, along with Bess who has been persuaded to change her mind by Maria.

ACT TWO

SCENE 2 Kittiwake Island, that evening. The picnickers dance and are entertained by Sportin' Life with his cynical song "It ain't necessarily so". Serena comes on the scene, denounces the company as sinners and reminds them it is time to board the ferryboat back to the dockside and Catfish Row. Bess lingers behind the others, and suddenly Crown appears before her. Despite her pleas to be let alone with Porgy, Crown's old fascination gradually overcomes her good intentions. The ferry leaves without her.

ACT TWO

SCENE 3 Jake and his fellow fishermen are preparing to put out to sea, Peter is back from prison and the voice of Bess, singing in delirium from Porgy's room, indicates that she, too, has returned after two days' absence. Serena and Porgy pray for Bess's recovery and soon she is on the mend. Porgy tells her he

LEFT The crippled Porgy's tenderness wins the heart of Bess, who eventually leaves her love, the stevedore Crown, to live with him.

RIGHT **Even though Bess has found happiness with Porgy, she is unable to resist Crown's fatal attractions when he returns and demands she take up their old relationship.**

knows that she was with Crown, but nevertheless he still loves her. Bess, for her part, begs him to protect her and he replies that she has no need to worry. He will take care of Crown if he dares to return. Clara meanwhile has been anxiously watching the sea and her fears are confirmed by the sound of the hurricane bell as the scene comes to an end.

ACT TWO SCENE 4 In Serena's room, everyone is praying, but their prayers are interrupted by a banging on the door. It is Crown. Porgy tries to protect Bess, but Crown hurls him to the floor. He sings a cheerful jazz song to counteract the gloomy praying, but suddenly, through the window, Clara sees Jake's boat floating upside down in the river. Leaving her child with Bess, she rushes out to find out what has happened, pleading for a man to go with her. Crown volunteers, but before leaving he promises Bess he will return for her. The rest of the company renew their prayers.

ACT THREE SCENE 1 Catfish Row is mourning Jake, Clara and Crown, all of whom are thought to have been killed in the storm. Sportin' Life mocks them, hinting that he knows Crown is not dead. Bess is heard singing Clara's lullaby to the baby, and slowly the assembled company drift off to bed.

Crown stealthily enters and picks his way across the court. As he passes Porgy's window, it opens and a hand emerges, holding a knife which is plunged into Crown's back. Crown staggers to his feet, but by now Porgy has him by the throat and throttles him to death.

ACT THREE SCENE 2 The police are on the scene, investigating Crown's murder. They question Serena and then Porgy, who is dragged off, protesting, to identify the body. Sportin' Life takes advantage of Bess's fears and

persuades her to accept some "dope" and again sings of the attractions of New York. He leaves a second packet of drugs behind him; after he has left, Bess snatches it up and takes it to Porgy's room.

ACT THREE SCENE 3 A week later. Things have returned to normal in Catfish Row and Porgy is greeted warmly as he returns from being imprisoned for contempt of court. He hands out presents, which he has bought with his winnings shooting craps in prison, but, when he asks for Bess, Serena and Maria tell him she has run away to New York with Sportin' Life. Porgy resolves to follow her and win her back. As he leaves the Row, a final spiritual is sung.

Leoncavallo (1858–1919)

I PAGLIACCI

Opera in two acts, libretto by the composer

***Ruggiero Leoncavallo
wrote more than 15
operas, including his
own version of* La
Bohème, *which,
unfortunately for him,
was premiered a year
after Puccini's
immortal masterpiece.
Only* I Pagliacci, *which
was an instant success
on its premiere in 1892,
has held its place in the
repertory because,
perhaps, Leoncavallo
remained true to the
verismo style.***

I PAGLIACCI (*The Clowns*) was first performed at the Teatro del Veme, Milan, on 21 May 1892. The first British performance took place in London in May 1893; the American première was staged in New York the following month.

Together with Pietro Mascagni, Leoncavallo was regarded as a leading member of the *verisimo* school of late 19th-century Italian opera. In common with other operas of this genre, *I Pagliacci* deals with an everyday situation – indeed, Leoncavallo based it on a real-life incident that took place in his childhood when his father, a local judge, tried a strolling player for the murder of his wife on-stage in exactly the same way as Canio kills Nedda. The opera was an instant success, but it was one that Leoncavallo was never to repeat. In performance, it is usually paired with another short opera, Mascagni's *Cavalleria Rusticana* (p 32).

PROLOGUE Tonio pokes his head through the theatre curtains – "Si puo?" ("By your permission") – and sets out the main themes of the opera that is to follow.

ACT ONE A bustling scene in the village of Montalto, in Calabria. It is the Feast of the Assumption, and the arrival of a band of strolling players is eagerly awaited. Beppe, costumed as Harlequin, enters leading a donkey, which is drawing a decorated cart in which Nedda reclines. Following them comes Canio, the head of the troupe, wearing his Pagliaccio costume, blowing a trumpet and beating a drum. Tonio, dressed as the clown Taddeo, brings up the rear. Canio promises the crowd that the performance will begin at seven that evening, then, angered by the fact that Tonio comes forward to help Nedda down, he boxes his ears before lifting his wife to the ground himself. Tonio goes off, muttering that he will get his own back on Canio.

CAST

Tonio
a clown (in the play Taddeo)
Baritone

Beppe
in the play Harlequin
Tenor

Nedda
Canio's wife (in the play Columbine)
Soprano

Canio
in the play Pagliaccio
Tenor

Silvio
a farmer
Baritone

Chorus
Villagers

A villager asks Canio for a drink, while another
teases him that Tonio is going to try to make love
to Nedda. Cannio is not amused – "Un falgioco
credetermi" ("Such a joke, believe me") – and
says that although he might have to put up with
this on the stage, anyone who tried to seduce
Nedda in real life had better beware. Slowly, as
the church bells ring, the villagers drift away, followed by Canio and Beppe.

Nedda, now alone, is disturbed. Can Canio suspect her? She is distracted, however, by the sound
of birdsong, and her thoughts go back to her
childhood. Tonio emerges from behind the im-
provised stage. He declares his love for Nedda,
but the more he pleads the more she mocks him,
until, as he tries to embrace her, she snatches up a
whip and slashes him across the face. Infuriated,
he runs off, swearing vengeance.

Another man's voice is heard calling Nedda's
name. It is Silvio, a local farmer and her lover.
Having reassured her that he has left Canio drinking in the tavern, he pleads with her to run away
with him after that evening's performance, and
eventually she yields. Their duet, however, has
been overheard by Tonio, who now brings Canio
back to the scene. As Silvio escapes, Canio demands
that his wife tell him the name of her lover. She

I Pagliacci

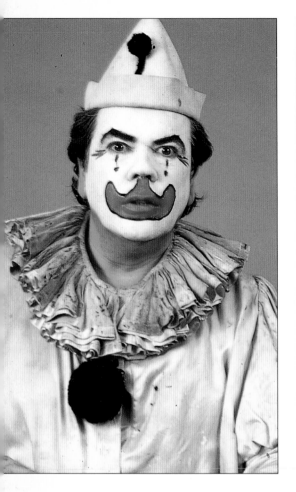

LEFT Nedda and Silvio sing of their love, but are interrupted by the returning Canio, who determines to discover the identity of his wife's lover and to avenge himself on his faithless wife.

FAR LEFT Grimly donning his costume, and applying his clown's make-up, Canio reflects, bitterly, that the show must go on. That night he must make his audience laugh, even though his heart is breaking.

OPPOSITE Canio has murdered his faithless wife, Nedda, and her lover, Silvio. The "comedy is finished".

refuses, and the furious Canio has to be physically restrained. Tonio counsels patience, saying that Nedda's lover will certainly be in their audience that evening and that a look or gesture is sure to give him away.

Canio, alone, starts to prepare for the performance. As he puts on his clown's make-up, he sings one of the best-known monologues in the whole of Italian opera, "Vesti la giubba" ("On with the motley"), with its climactic outburst "Ridi, Pagliaccio" ("Laugh, Pagliaccio … even though your heart is breaking").

ACT TWO As the audience gathers, Nedda, in her Columbine costume, goes around collecting the ticket money. She sees Silvio and mutters a warning to him. A bell rings and the play begins. Columbine is waiting impatiently for Harlequin, her lover, who eventually serenades her through an open window. It is Taddeo who enters, how-

ever. He makes grotesque advances to Columbine, who signals to Harlequin to rescue her. He climbs through the window and kicks Taddeo off the stage.

The lovers plot to drug Pagliaccio so that they can flee together. Taddeo bursts in with the news that Pagliaccio is returning, full of suspicion that he has been betrayed. Harlequin escapes, while Taddeo hides in a cupboard.

Pagliaccio cross-questions Columbine, and as the questioning becomes more and more intense, Nedda realizes that Canio is no longer acting but in deadly earnest. As he repeatedly demands her lover's name, the audience, too, realizes that something is amiss. Canio snatches up a knife and, as Nedda tries to escape into the crowd, he stabs her. With her last breath, she cries out to Silvio for help. As Silvio calls back to her in his despair, Canio strikes again and Silvio falls dead by Nedda's side. Turning to the terrified villagers, Canio announces that the "comedy is over", ("La commedia è finita").

Mascagni (1863–1945)

CAVALLERIA RUSTICANA

Opera in one act, libretto by Guido Menasci and Giuseppe Targioni-Tozzeti, based on a short story by Giovanni Verga

With Cavalleria Rusticana, *which won instant success on its first performance in 1890, Pietro Mascagni established verismo as an influential force on the operatic stage. He wrote the opera as an entry for a competition, in which it won the first prize; however, his later operas, such as the monumental* Nerone, *never recaptured its success, although some – notably* L'Amico Fritz *– have fine musical qualities.*

CAVALLERIA *Rusticana (Rustic Chivalry)* was first performed at the Teatro Constanzi, Rome, on 17 May 1890. Its American première was at Philadelphia the following year, while the first British performance was at the Shaftesbury Theatre, London.

Cavalleria Rusticana is a Sicilian drama *par excellence*. It is full of swift action, deep emotion, passion, betrayal and revenge. Its immediate success made the 26-year-old Mascagni world famous, but, try as he might, he was never again able to achieve the same heights throughout his long career, which extended into the gramophone age. In 1940, to mark the opera's 50th anniversary, he recorded it with a classic cast in Rome.

The opera starts with a short, passionate prelude, as part of which we hear a serenade sung to Lola by Turridu behind the curtain. On the prelude's conclusion, the curtain rises to reveal the main square of a Sicilian village on Easter morning. People bustle about, the church bells ring and a chorus follows. The crowd disperses, leaving the sad figure of Santuzza alone on the stage. She approaches Mamma Lucia's house as the latter is emerging and asks for Turridu. On being told that he has gone to a neighbouring town to buy wine, she replies that this cannot be so because he was seen in the village during the night. Mamma Lucia asks her in, but she refuses, for she is excommunicate.

As Mamma Lucia starts to cross-question Santuzza, the women are interrupted by the cracking of a whip and the jingling of harness bells off-stage. These herald the arrival of Alfio, accompanied by the villagers. He sings the praises of a teamster's life and of his wife's beauty, going on to confirm that Turridu has been around the village. He himself saw him that morning, not too far from his cottage.

CAST

Santuzza
a village girl
Soprano

Lucia
Turridu's mother
Contralto

Alfio
a carter
Baritone

Turridu
a young soldier
Tenor

Lola
Alfio's wife
Mezzo-soprano

Chorus
Villagers

As Alfio leaves, the church choir, off-stage, in-tones the *Regina Coeli*, and the villagers in the square respond with fervent Allelujas. They kneel and, led by Santuzza, join in the great Easter hymn before making their way into the church. Mamma Lucia asks Santuzza why she signalled to her to keep silent when Alfio spoke of Turridu's presence in the village, and Santuzza tells the story of her seduction and betrayal. Before Turridu left for military service, he and Lola were lovers, but, tir-ing of waiting, the flighty Lola married Alfio. On his return, Turridu seduced Santuzza, but, egged on by Lola, he has now returned to his first love. Lucia pities the girl, who implores her to go into the church and pray for her.

Turridu enters. Santuzza upbraids him for his faithlessness, but her mood soon changes to one of forgiveness. At that moment, however, Lola is heard singing off-stage. She enters, mocks Santuzza and goes into the church. Turridu makes to follow, but Santuzza, in one of the most moving moments of the entire opera, begs him to stay. Eventually he flings her to the ground and goes after Lola.

Alfio enters and Santuzza sees her chance for revenge. She tells him about his wife's affair with Turridu, and he swears vengeance on his wife's seducer.

ABOVE It is Easter morning, and the villagers are in holiday mood. They join the church choir in the great Easter hymn, led by Santuzza.

RIGHT Santuzza pours out the sad story of her betrayal by her lover, Turridu, to his mother, Lucia. She still loves him, she sings, even though he has abandoned her for another.

A short orchestral *intermezzo* leads to the final scene. Church is over, and Turridu leads the vil-lagers in a drinking song. Alfio enters, refuses to drink with Turridu and eventually challenges him to a duel, Alfio leaves and Turridu says farewell to his mother, in an aria that is almost a premonition of death. He runs after Alfio. The stage fills until, from afar, a woman's voice is heard calling that Turridu has been killed. The cry is repeated. Santuzza collapses and the curtain falls.

WOLFGANG AMADEUS *Mozart* (1756–91)

LE NOZZE DI FIGARO

Opera buffa *in four acts, libretto by Lorenzo da Ponte after the play by Pierre Beaumarchais*

Wolfgang Amadeus Mozart started composing at the age of five; in addition to 13 full-scale operas, he wrote 41 symphonies, over 40 concertos and 26 string quartets, songs and other chamber works. Among his many gifts was an outstanding memory; as a child prodigy, he managed to write out the whole of Allegri's celebrated Miserere, publication of which was forbidden by the Popes, after hearing it only twice on a visit to Rome.

L E NOZZE *di Figaro (The Marriage of Figaro)* was first performed at the Burgtheater, Vienna, on 1 May 1786. The first British performance was at the Haymarket Theatre, London, in 1812; the American première took place in New York in 1824. Mozart's happiest opera was only a partial success on its first performance. The Emperor Joseph II complained that it had "too many notes" and "was not meat for my Viennese". Modern audiences, however, regard the opera a miracle of dramatic and musical construction, the only exceptions being the showpiece arias Mozart wrote for Marcellina and Basilio in Act 4, which do not advance the action and are customarily cut.

ACT ONE After a bustling overture the curtain rises on a semi-furnished room in Count Almaviva's country castle. Figaro is measuring up the floor, while Susanna is trying on a new hat, which she intends to wear at their forthcoming wedding. When Figaro tells her that, thanks to the generosity of the Count, these are to be their new quarters, she tells him there is more to this generosity than meets the eye. Even though the Count has abolished the feudal custom of the *droit de seigneur*, he intends to re-establish it through her. She goes off in response to the Countess's bell and Figaro is left alone to contemplate this unwelcome news. He swears that he will outwit his master.

No sooner has Figaro left the stage than Dr Bartolo and his housekeeper, Marcellina, enter. Bartolo has not forgiven Figaro for helping the Count elope with the Countess, who was once his ward, and he has encouraged Marcellina to bring a legal case against him: Figaro will either have to pay her back the money he has borrowed from her or marry her. Bartolo sings of the delights of vengeance, before going off to confer with the Count. As Marcellina makes to follow him, she

CAST

Figaro
Count Almaviva's valet
Baritone

Susanna
the Countess Almaviva's maid
Soprano

Marcellina
housekeeper to Dr Bartolo
Mezzo-soprano

Dr Bartolo
Bass

Cherubino
a page
Soprano

Count Almaviva
Baritone

Don Basilio
a music teacher
Tenor

Countess Almaviva
Soprano

Antonio
head gardener
Bass

Don Curzio
a lawyer
Tenor

Barbarina
Antonio's daughter
Soprano

Chorus
Peasants on Almaviva's estate

ABOVE Figaro and Susanna are happily preparing for their wedding. But Susanna reveals that their master, Count Almaviva, is plotting to reinstate the feudal *droit de seigneur*, although he has supposedly abolished the ancient custom.

ABOVE RIGHT The Count declares his feelings for Susanna, unaware that Cherubino is listening in concealment.

collides with the returning Susanna, and they exchange insults in a brief duet.

Marcellina flounces out, discomfited, and Cherubino enters, imploring Susanna to intercede with the Countess and get him reinstated as the Count's page (the Count has dismissed him for flirting with Barbarina). He breathlessly sings of the attraction all women have for him – "Non so più" ("Is it pain or pleasure that fills me?"). No sooner has he finished than two male voices are heard outside, and Susanna hides him as the Count himself enters. He starts to flirt with her, but, when Basilio is heard approaching, he, too, hides.

Basilio teases Susanna about Cherubino, but, when he says that everyone is talking about the page's infatuation with the Countess, the Count bursts out of concealment. In the trio that follows, Susanna pretends to faint, but revives in time to plead Cherubino's case. He is only a boy, she says, but the Count replies by telling her how he found him hiding the previous day in Barbarina's room. He draws the dust sheet off a chair to demonstrate the discovery and reveals – Cherubino. He tells Basilio to fetch Figaro immediately, but is halted in his tracks when he realizes that Cherubino has overheard his conversation with Susanna.

ABOVE The Count discovers the young page Cherubino concealed in a chair. Angrily he orders him to leave to take up a commission in his regiment.

LEFT Accompanied by Susanna, Cherubino serenades the Countess with the song he has specially composed in her honour.

OPPOSITE Susanna starts to dress Cherubino in women's clothes, but the intended masquerade is interrupted by the inopportune arrival of the Count, full of jealousy and suspicion.

Figaro and the chorus enter and, after a salutation is sung to the Count, he joins Susanna and Cherubino in their pleadings. The Count responds by appointing the page to a commission in his regiment and tells him to leave at once. Figaro speeds the reluctant page on his way with a spirited description of the rigours that await him in the army, in the aria "Non piu andrai" ("Bid farewell to a life of pleasure").

ACT TWO The antechamber to the Countess's bedroom. In the aria "Porgi amor" ("God of love") the Countess sings sadly of her frustrated love for her husband. Susanna comforts her and then admits Figaro, who tells the Countess of the plan he has devised. Susanna will make an assignation with the Count but it will be kept by Cherubino, disguised as a girl, while Figaro, for his part, will alert the Count through an anonymous note that the Countess has an assignation of her own.

Cherubino enters to be dressed for his part, but first he sings a song he has written to honour the Countess, his god-mother, "Voi che sapete" ("Tell me, fair ladies"). He and Susanna sing a lively duet as he tries on his lady's clothes. A knock is heard at the locked door. It is the Count, who has received Figaro's anonymous note. Cherubino locks himself in the Countess's bedroom while Susanna hides behind a curtain. The Count searches the room and demands that the locked door be opened. The Countess refuses to allow this, saying that Susanna is within, trying on her wedding dress. The Count drags her off in search of tools to break down the door, locking the ante-chamber door behind them. Susanna and Cherubino breathlessly emerge from their hiding places, and as the Count is heard returning, Cherubino jumps out of the window, while Susanna takes his place.

By now, the Count is in an evil temper, a temper that is not improved when his wife confesses that it is Cherubino, rather than Susanna, who is in hiding. He launches the great finale, one of the longest Mozart ever wrote, with a curt order for Cherubino to come out at once. His fury mounts as the Countess continues her pleading, only to turn to complete amazement when the door opens and Susanna emerges. As the Count vainly searches for the page, the women quickly confer and, when he re-enters, take advantage of his confusion to make him beg forgiveness. They even manage to explain away the anonymous note, which they reveal was written by Figaro. At this moment, Figaro himself enters and the Count's suspicions are re-awakened, especially when, despite desperate hints from the Countess and Susanna, Figaro denies all knowledge of it. They tell him that the joke is over and the Count is temporarily pacified.

Now, however, the aggrieved Antonio bursts into the room, carrying a broken flower-pot. He tells the Count he is used to being abused, but it is the last straw when men jump out of windows and damage his flowers. Figaro says the figure Antonio saw was him, but Antonio thinks it looked more like Cherubino. If it was Figaro, he had better return him a letter the fugitive dropped. The Count snatches the letter from Antonio and asks the non-plussed Figaro what it is. Just in time, the Countess recognizes it as Cherubino's commission, which needs the Count's seal on it to make it legal, and she and Susanna prompt Figaro in whispered asides.

Figaro's triumph is short-lived, however. Dr Bartello, Marcellina and their lawyer, Don Curzio, enter to demand justice, along with Basilio as a leading witness. The Count decides there is a case to answer and the act ends in complete confusion.

ACT THREE The Count is mulling over the
SCENE 1 events of the day, when Susanna enters on the pretext of borrowing his smelling-salts for her mistress. In reality, she says, she has come to arrange to meet him that night in the castle gardens. As she leaves, she meets Figaro and assures him that, without a lawyer, she has won her case. Unfortunately, the Count has overheard and in the aria "Vedrò mentr'io sospiro" ("Must I renounce my pleasure?") gives full vent to his feelings. He promptly gives judgement for Marcellina – pay her or marry her – but Figaro says that, although a foundling, he is well-born and cannot marry without the consent of his parents. When he reveals his possession of a strawberry birthmark, Marcellina realizes he is her long-lost illegitimate son and reveals, too, that Bartolo is his father. As the three embrace and the Count gives vent to his frustration, Susanna enters with the money to pay the debt, which she has secured from the Countess. Bewildered and angered by what is going on, she promptly boxes Figaro's ears, but eventually all is explained.

ACT THREE The Countess is alone. She sings
SCENE 2 of her former happiness in the aria "Dove Sóno" ("Happy days, now long departed"), and then is joined by Susanna. The Countess dictates a note to her, confirming arrangements for the assignation, and the two agree to exchange clothes, the Countess keeping the rendezvous dressed as her maid.

A chorus of peasant girls enters and presents the Countess with flowers. She remarks to Susanna how familiar one of them looks. The Count and Antonio enter and unmask the "girl" as Cherubino. Barbarina comes to her sweetheart's rescue, reminding the Count how often he has promised her anything she wanted. The discomfited Count and the outraged Countess prepare to greet the happy couples (it is now a dual wedding, Bartolo having agreed to marry Marcellina), and, as a dance strikes up, Susanna manages to pass the Count her letter, which she has sealed with a pin. As Figaro notices, this pricks the Count's fingers as he opens the note. He announces a splendid feast, complete with fireworks, in honour of the marriages, and the act ends with a chorus in his honour.

WOLFGANG AMADEUS MOZART

....

Le Nozze di Figaro

RIGHT Convinced that Susanna is, after all, about to betray him with the Count, Figaro warns all husbands of the dangers of the cuckold's horns.

LEFT All ends happily as the discomfited Count pleads for his wife's forgiveness and the entire cast sings of the follies of the day.

ACT FOUR Barbarina is searching the garden for Susanna's pin, which the Count gave her to return, but which she has dropped. Figaro comes in with Marcellina and is overcome by this apparent evidence of Susanna's treachery. Swearing vengeance on her, he storms off in search of witnesses, while Marcellina goes off to warn Susanna – she may be guilty or innocent, but all women should stick together. Figaro returns with Bartolo and Basilio, telling them to remain close at hand to witness Susanna's seduction by the Count. In a long aria, he sings of the folly of trusting a woman.

Susanna and the Countess enter. She asks her mistress if she can stay in the garden to enjoy the night air. Knowing full well that Figaro is concealed within earshot, she sings of her longing for her noble lover – "Deh vieni non tardar" ("Then come, my beloved"). At this point, Cherubino enters and the second great finale begins. Taking the Countess for Susanna (it is dark and the two have exchanged cloaks), he tries to flirt with her, only to run off as the Count approaches. Almaviva is equally deceived; as Figaro storms across the stage in a fury, the two conceal themselves in different parts of the garden.

Figaro is singing of his lost honour when Susanna, dressed as the Countess, calls to him. He starts to appeal to her for justice, but, when she lets her assumed voice slip for a moment, realizes he is addressing his own wife. It is his chance to pay her back, and he starts to make love to her, only desisting when the indignant Susanna reveals herself. He says he had already recognized her by her voice – the voice he adores.

The Count re-enters, looking for the false Susanna, and Figaro is let in on the great secret. The two decide to take the joke a stage further forward and begin to flirt passionately, to the fury of the Count. Grasping hold of Figaro as Susanna makes good her escape, he calls to anyone within hearing to bear witness to his wife's disgrace and pulls in turn from their hiding places Cherubino, Barbarina, Marcellina and, finally, the supposed Countess. All plead for forgiveness, but he remains adamant, until the voice of the Countess, still disguised as Susanna, adds itself to the plea as she re-enters. It is the dumbfounded Count's turn to beg his wife for pardon, which she grants. The opera ends in general rejoicing.

DON GIOVANNI

Opera in two acts, libretto by Lorenzo da Ponte

CAST

Leporello
Don Giovanni's valet
Bass

Don Giovanni
Baritone

Donna Anna
Soprano

The Commendatore
her father
Bass

Don Ottavio
Donna Anna's
fiancée
Tenor

Donna Elvira
Soprano

Zerlina
Soprano

Masetto
Zerlina's fiancé
Bass

Chorus
Peasants, retainers,
musicians

LEFT Leporello tells the indignant Donna Elvira that she is but one of a catalogue of women whom Don Giovanni has seduced – in Spain alone, a thousand and three have fallen victim to his charms.

Don *Giovanni* was first performed at the National Theatre, Prague, on 29 October 1787. The first performance in Britain was at His Majesty's Theatre, London, on 12 April 1819; the opera, retitled *The Libertine*, was first performed in America, in Philadelphia, the following year.

Although *Figaro* had not been a total success in Vienna, it was a triumph in Prague, and the theatre there was quick to commission Mozart to write a new opera. Since then, *Don Giovanni* has constantly held the stage, although for much of the 19th century not in the form that is familiar to us today. The final "moral" was usually cut, the opera ending with what Bernard Shaw condemned as the "sensational vulgarity" of bringing down the curtain as the statue of the Commendatore carries the Don down to hell amid clouds of flame.

ACT ONE
SCENE 1
The overture leads straight into the first scene. Leporello is discovered singing of the misery of a servant's life. "Notte e giorno faticar" ("Day and night I'm on the go"). He has been left on guard while his master is attempting the seduction of Donna Anna, the Commendatore's daughter, but his litany of complaints is interrupted by the arrival of Don Giovanni, hotly pursued by Donna Anna. As the two struggle, with Leporello adding his comments, the noise brings the Commendatore to the scene. Giovanni and the Commendatore fight a duel, and the Commendatore falls, mortally wounded. Don Giovanni and Leporello make good their escape as Donna Anna, who has gone in search of help, returns with her fiancé, Don Ottavio. He tries to comfort her, but in vain. They both swear vengeance on the unknown assassin.

WOLFGANG AMADEUS MOZART

....

Don Giovanni

RIGHT Whether celebrating the joys of life, as in the "champagne" aria, or defying death in the finale, Don Giovanni is the archetypal rake and bon vivant.

LEFT The Don's relationship with Zerlina is ambivalent from the moment he meets her. Despite her protestations, it seems extremely likely that, if he were left alone with her uninterrupted, Leporello would have another entry to make in his catalogue of his master's conquests.

ACT ONE Giovanni and Leporello are on the prowl on the streets of Seville, when

SCENE 2 a veiled woman enters, fresh from a long journey. She denounces her faithless lover in the aria "Ah chi mi dice mai" ("Where shall I find the traitor?"), while Don Giovanni prepares to console her. As he approaches, she lifts her veil, and he sees it is Donna Elvira, whom he himself has deceived and betrayed. Giovanni parries her accusations, telling her that Leporello can explain

everything, but as Leporello stammers a halting sentence or two, he makes his escape. Free of his master's presence, Leporello tells Donna Elvira she is lucky to be rid of him; she is only one of a catalogue of conquests the Don has made across Europe – "Madamina" ("Let me tell you"). He, too, runs off, and Elvira retires to a nearby inn, swearing vengeance on Don Giovanni.

A wedding party enters, celebrating the coming marriage of Zerlina, a pretty peasant girl, to Masetto. Don Giovanni, seeing the chance of another conquest, orders Leporello to take the entire party, excepting, of course, Zerlina, to his nearby palace, where he will entertain them. Masetto protests – "Ho capito, Signor" ("I understand exactly") – but Zerlina, her head already turned by the Don's flattery, tells him she will be perfectly safe. Left alone with Zerlina, Giovanni quickly capitalizes on the situation and, despite a momentary hesitation, Zerlina is quick to fall victim to his charms, as they sing together "Là ci darem la mano" ("Let me take your hand").

Donna Elvira re-enters. She denounces Giovanni and takes Zerlina away with her – "Ah, fuggi il traditor" ("Flee from this traitor") – leaving the frustrated Don to face Donna Anna and Don Ottavio, who have come to seek his help. No sooner has he started talking with them than Donna

RIGHT **Leporello greets Donna Anna, Donna Elvira and Don Ottavio. When they unmask themselves, however, it is to accuse Don Giovanni of murder and treachery. As the entire company round on him, the Don is discomfited at first, but quickly recovers his nerve to make good his escape.**

Elvira returns. She tells the bewildered couple that Giovanni is a heartless deceiver. He tries to pass off the situation by telling them she is deranged, eventually dragging her off the stage. The two do not know who to believe until Donna Anna suddenly realizes, from the sound of the Don's voice, that he was her attempted seducer and her father's murderer. She relives the events of that dreadful night, and Don Ottavio again swears that he will take up the burden of vengeance.

RIGHT **Don Ottavio asks Donna Elvira to look after Donna Anna while he goes to secure a warrant for Don Giovanni's arrest. The aria he sings is one of the most moving that Mozart ever wrote.**

ACT ONE
SCENE 3

Don Giovanni and Leporello compare notes. Everything is going badly, says Leporello, but the Don disagrees. Nothing could be better. He orders the celebrations to go ahead as planned – "Fin ch'han dal vino" ("Let the wine flow").

Meanwhile, Masetto and Zerlina are making up their quarrel – "Batti, batti, O bel Masetto" ("Beat me, chide me") – but Masetto's suspicions are reawakened when they hear Giovanni's voice in the distance. He hides as the Don enters to order his retainers to make sure that the evening is a success, and he confronts the couple as the Don leads Zerlina off. Giovanni is ready with an explanation – he was taking Zerlina to look for Masetto – and he takes them both to the palace, where dancing is about to begin. Donna Elvira, Donna Anna and

Don Ottavio appear, cloaked and masked. Leporello sees them from a window and, on his master's orders, asks them to join the party. Don Ottavio accepts, and the three raise their masks and pray to God to protect them in their mission.

ACT ONE
SCENE 4

Inside the palace ballroom, festivities are in full swing. The three masked figures enter and are greeted by the company, after which the dancing

Don Giovanni

LEFT Don Giovanni orders the terrified Leporello to invite the statue of the murdered Commendatore to supper, but even he is taken aback when the statue responds with the single word "si!" ("Yes!").

OPPOSITE LEFT The Commendatore's statue arrives in response to Don Giovanni's rash invitation to dinner with a counter-offer – for the Don to dine with him.

starts. Don Giovanni orders Leporello to distract Masetto, while he makes off with Zerlina. Suddenly, a piercing scream is heard off-stage and a dishevelled Zerlina rushes in, followed by the Don, sword in hand and leading Leporello by the ear. He claims that Leporello is the seducer, but, as Donna Anna, Donna Elvira and Don Ottavio reveal themselves and denounce him, no one is deceived. Taken aback at first, Don Giovanni quickly recovers and makes his escape as the curtain falls.

ACT TWO Back outside Donna Elvira's inn, Don Giovanni and Leporello are
SCENE 1 arguing – "Eh, via buffone" ("Go, you rascal") – but master eventually pacifies servant with a purse of gold. He tells Leporello that his new target is Donna Elvira's maid. His plan is that the two will change clothes, and the disguised Leporello will lure Donna Elvira away. The luckless valet mimes his way as the Don through a trio, pleading for forgiveness, but perks up when Donna Elvira starts embracing him. Don Giovanni frightens the two off and serenades his new love – "Deh, vieni alla finestra" ("O come to the window") – only to be interrupted by Masetto and a gang of armed peasants, who are intent on finding and killing Giovanni. They take the disguised Don for Leporello, and he promises to help them, split-

ting the band up and sending its members in different directions – "Meta di voi qua vadano" ("Some go that way") – until he and Masetto are alone. He beats Masetto up and runs off, laughing. Masetto's groans attract Zerlina, who consoles him and helps him away – "Vedrai, carino" ("Come, my beloved").

ACT TWO A palace courtyard. Donna Elvira
SCENE 2 and the still-disguised Leporello enter. As Donna Elvira sings of her rekindled love, Leporello tries to sneak away but is stopped by the arrival of, first, Donna Anna and Don Ottavio and then of Zerlina and Masetto. Despite Donna Elvira's pleas for clemency, the company calls for his death, until, to save himself, Leporello throws off his disguise and begs for mercy, sidling towards a doorway through which he eventually makes a successful getaway. Don Ottavio asks Donna Elvira to care for Donna Anna – "Il mio tesoro" ("Watch over my love") – while he goes off to obtain a warrant for Don Giovanni's arrest. Donna Elvira, however, is still torn by mixed feelings – "Mi tradi" ("Once betrayed").

ACT TWO A churchyard. The Don exclaims
SCENE 3 how bright the night is – it is almost as light as day – as Leporello enters, again complaining. To cheer him up,

BELOW Don Giovanni takes the Commendatore's hand whereupon he exclaims that the latter's touch has turned his blood to ice. Despite the Commendatore's appeals for Don Giovanni's repentance – enjoined by Leporello – the defiant Don is dragged down into Hell.

Giovanni tells him of his latest conquest, a girl he met in the street who took him for his servant. Leporello indignantly asks what would have happened if she had been his daughter. "Even better," replies the Don, but, to the sound of off-stage trombones, a solemn voice is heard telling him to leave the dead in peace. The Don orders Leporello to investigate and the latter discovers a statue of the Commendatore. The Don orders the terrified Leporello to invite the statue to supper, but even he is nonplussed when he repeats the invitation himself, and the statue replies with "Si" ("Yes!").

ACT TWO
SCENE 4 The scene reverts to Donna Anna's palace. Don Ottavio begs her to name their wedding day, but she replies she can think of nothing but her dead father – "Non mir dir" ("Do not ask me").

ACT TWO
SCENE 5 Seated in his palace, the Don is about to start supper, served by Leporello and accompanied by a stage wind band, which plays popular tunes from other operas of the day, including *The Marriage of Figaro*. Leporello steals a morsel of chicken, but is forced to own up to his theft. Donna Elvira enters to make a last plea to the Don to repent, but the heartless Giovanni mocks her once more. She leaves in despair, but then her scream is heard in the corridor. Giovanni sends Leporello to investigate, but he returns in terror with the news that the Commendatore's statue is on the march, approaching the palace door. The exasperated Don goes to look for himself, but at that moment, the statue enters. Gravely, the Commendatore thanks the Don for his invitation and, in return, asks Giovanni to dine with him. Despite Leporello's entreaties, the Don defiantly consents and clasps the Commendatore's stone hand. The fires of Hell rise and, refusing to the last to repent, the Don is dragged down to meet his doom.

The entire company now burst on to the scene in search of the Don, and the terrified Leporello tells them of heaven's retribution. In a final ensemble, they moralize on Don Giovanni's justified fate – "Questo é il fin di chi fa mal" ("Sinner, pause and ponder well").

COSÌ FAN TUTTE

Opera buffa in two acts, libretto by Lorenzo da Ponte

CAST

Ferrando
Dorabella's fiancé
Tenor

Guglielmo
Fiordiligi's fiancé
Bass

Don Alfonso
a cynical philosopher
Baritone

Fiordiligi
Soprano

Dorabella
her sister
Soprano

Despina
the sisters' maid
Soprano

Chorus
Local inhabitants,
servants

LEFT Don Alfonso introduces his Albanian friends to Fiordiligi and Dorabella, whom they quickly offend with their elaborate protestations of love.

Cosi *fan tutte (Women are All Alike)* was first performed at the Burgtheater, Vienna, on 26 January 1790; the first performance in Britain was at the Haymarket Theatre, London in 1811.

Così fan tutte, Mozart's last great comic opera, came into its own only in the current century. Throughout the Victorian era it was scarcely performed, unlike *Le Nozze di Figaro* and *Don Giovanni*, which always remained in the repertory. The reason for this neglect lay in its plot, which the Victorians regarded as immoral.

ACT ONE
SCENE 1 As the curtain rises, Ferrando and Guglielmo, two officers, are discovered arguing with their friend Don Alfonso about the fidelity of women. Both claim that their loves are incapable of betraying them. Don Alfonso, on the other hand, cynically asserts that any woman's loyalty is as mythical as the fabled phoenix. The outraged duo agree to put their belief to the test: for a wager of a hundred guineas, Alfonso swears that he will prove their fiancées unfaithful, provided the two lovers agree to do exactly as he tells them. Ferrando and Guglielmo debate how they will spend their winnings: Ferrando will arrange a serenade and Guglielmo a banquet, to which Alfonso naturally will be invited, since he will have to pay the bill.

ACT ONE
SCENE 2 A room in the sisters' home. Fiordiligi and Dorabella are admiring their lockets, each of which carries a portrait of her lover, when Alfonso hurries in with bad news. The men, he says, have been called to the colours and must leave immediately. Ferrando and Guglielmo enter and the lovers bid each other an emotional farewell, while

Alfonso comments cynically on the sidelines. A march strikes up and the two men leave for war. In a flowing, gentle trio, Alfonso and the two sisters pray for a safe journey and return. Once alone, however, Alfonso mocks the stupidity of wasting money on a woman's inevitably fickle emotions.

Despina, the sisters' maid, enters with some hot chocolate, which she is about to sample, when they both burst in, overcome with grief and despair. Dorabella is particularly vehement in her protestations, but Despina counsels her employers not to be stupid – now is their chance to make hay while the sun shines. They leave in disgust. This is the cue for Alfonso to appear and enlist Despina's aid on behalf of two foreign friends of his, whom he wants to introduce to Fiordiligi and Dorabella. Enter Ferrando and Guglielmo, so heavily and effectively disguised as Albanians that Despina totally fails to recognize them. So, too, do the sisters when they return. They indignantly order the intruders out of the house.

Alfonso emerges to welcome the Albanians as his oldest and dearest friends. They promptly swamp the sisters with elaborate declarations of

LEFT "Come scoglio" ("Firm as a rock"), sings Dorabella, describing her love for Ferrando. In fact, she is relatively quick to succumb to the attractions of the disguised Guglielmo.

BELOW Confronted by the two, supposedly poisoned, Albanians, Dorabella is torn by conflicting emotions.

LEFT Despina, the sisters' maid, is quick to urge them to take advantage of their lovers' absence and enjoy themselves to the full. It is, she tells them, unlikely that a man would be faithful in similar circumstances.

RIGHT Fiordiligi seems to be made of sterner stuff. She decides to disguise herself and go in search of her lover, but Ferrando finally breaks down her resistance by asking her to stab him through the heart.

love, which spark Fiordiligi into a storm of righteous indignation – "Come scoglio" ("Firm as a rock"). In response, Guglielmo catalogues his and Ferrando's attractions down to their moustaches, but before he can finish, the sisters stalk off, followed by Despina. Although all three men collapse in laughter, Alfonso reminds his friends that he still has time to win the bet. He goes off as Ferrando sings of his love for Dorabella.

ACT ONE
SCENE 3 In the garden of their villa the sisters are pining for their endangered lovers when the Albanians rush in, declaring that, because of their rejection, there is no future for them but death. Despite Alfonso's efforts to restrain them, they promptly swallow what appears to be poison. In response to the sisters' calls for help, Despina promptly appears and is sent off to fetch a doctor. The sisters feel for the victims' pulses, but all seems lost.

At this moment, however, the "doctor" arrives – it is Despina in disguise. She proclaims herself a disciple of the great Mesmer and, with the aid of a giant magnet, mesmerizes the Albanians back to life. Staring into the sisters' eyes, they declare they must have reached Heaven to be greeted by two such goddesses. Unfortunately, they go one step too far by asking for a kiss. The act ends with the sisters indignantly defending their honour, cynical comment from Alfonso and Despina and, as an aside, approval for the sisters' protestations from the Albanians themselves.

ACT TWO
SCENE 1 Despina urges her employers to make the most of the handsome strangers while their lovers are away – "Una donna a quindici anni", she sings ("even a girl of 15 would know what to do"), and the sisters decide that perhaps a mild flirtation would do no harm after all, debating which they prefer. Dorabella expresses a preference for the disguised Guglielmo, while Fiordiligi opts for the disguised Ferrando.

ACT TWO
SCENE 2 The sound of a serenade is heard; the Albanians have arranged this salute to help them win their new loves. Despite encouragement from Alfonso and Despina, however, the four are too tongue-tied to speak, making polite conversation about the weather, until Fiordiligi breaks the ice by taking Ferrando off for a stroll. Left alone with Dorabella, Guglielmo succeeds in breaking down her resistance, exchanging lockets.

RIGHT The Albanians and sisters prepare to solemnise their betrothal, but there are more shocks in store.

Ferrando and Fiordiligi return, but he is rebuffed. (Ferrando's aria, "Ah lo veggio" is usually cut in modern performances.) Once alone, Fiordiligi sings of her conflicting emotions – "Per pieta, ben mio, perdona" ("Forgive me, my beloved") – resolving to resist temptation.

The gleeful Ferrando tells Guglielmo the bet is as good as won, but his joy turns to consternation when Guglielmo shows him the locket and reveals he has succeeded. Echoing the words of Alfonso, he urges Ferrando not to take it too much to heart, who curses Dorabella for her faithlessness.

ACT TWO SCENE 3 Despina congratulates Dorabella on her success, but Fiordiligi is furious with her sister – and possibly herself. She urges loyalty, but Dorabella replies that love's fancies must be obeyed. Fiordiligi decides on a last, desperate plan. She and Dorabella will disguise themselves as soldiers and join their lovers on the battlefield. But she is interrupted by Ferrando, who, observed by Guglielmo and Alfonso from concealment, finally succeeds in winning her love. Guglielmo rages at Alfonso and the now-triumphant Ferrando, but Alfonso reminds them that it is not really their fiancées' fault. All women are equally fickle – "Così fan tutte".

ACT TWO SCENE 4 Alfonso and Despina, together with a chorus of servants, are making the final preparations for the betrothal of the sisters to the Albanians. The couples toast each other, Guglielmo muttering that he wishes the wine would turn to poison, before the arrival of a notary (Despina in another disguise). As the marriage contract is signed, the march that was heard in the first act strikes up – Ferrando and Guglielmo are returning from the wars. In feigned panic, the Albanians rush off and Despina hides.

Ferrando and Guglielmo re-enter, undisguised. They discover the hidden notary, but Despina, too, removes her disguise, claiming to have just been returning from a fancy-dress ball. Then they discover the marriage contract, which Alfonso deliberately lets fall, and this leads to accusations and admissions of guilt. Alfonso tells the indignant men that the proof they are seeking lies in the next room. They march out, to return immediately carrying bits of their Albanian disguises. As the whole plot is revealed, the sisters round indignantly on Alfonso, but he tells them not to blame him – he simply wanted to rid all four of them of their romantic illusions – but to kiss and make up. A final ensemble, praising anyone with the ability to take the rough with the smooth, ends the opera.

WOLFGANG AMADEUS
MOZART

DIE ZAUBERFLÖTE

Opera in two acts, libretto by Emanuel Schikaneder

LEFT **Tamino, lost in the forest, battles for his life against a serpent before falling to the ground in a faint.**

CAST

Tamino
a prince
Tenor

Three ladies
in the service of the
Queen of Night
*Soprano, soprano,
mezzo-soprano*

Papageno
a bird catcher
Baritone

**The Queen of
Night**
Soprano

Monostatos
a Moor in the service
of Sarastro
Tenor

Pamina
the Queen of Night's
daughter
Soprano

Three wise boys
*Soprano, soprano,
mezzo-soprano*

**The Speaker of the
temple**
Bass

Sarastro
high priest of Isis
and Osiris
Bass

Two Priests
Tenor, bass

Papagena
Soprano

**Two men in
armour**
Tenor, bass

Chorus
Priests, people

LEFT **Papageno, half-man and half-bird, celebrates the delights of being a "jolly birdcatcher".**

BELOW **The Queen of Night sings of her grief at the loss of her daughter to the "evil magician" Sarastro. Rescue Pamina, she promises Tamino, and he will be rewarded with the princess's hand.**

DIE *Zauberflöte (The Magic Flute)* was first performed at the Theater an der Wien, Vienna, on 30 September 1791; its first British performance was at the Haymarket Theatre, London, in 1811.

With *Die Zauberflöte*, Mozart returned to the German *singspiel* style he had adopted in his early opera *Die Entführung aus dem Serail (The Abduction from the Seraglio)* and with the same success. Schikaneder, his librettist and the original Papageno, was a considerable showman, and he persuaded Mozart that such an opera would appeal to the ordinary Viennese and bring in the money of which the impoverished composer was in such need. Much has been written of the symbolism that may lie behind the story – whether, for instance, the rituals of the priests and their search for wisdom and truth mirror those of Freemasonry (both Schikaneder and Mozart were Masons), and whether the character of the Queen of Night is based on that of Maria Theresa, who, as Empress of Austria, had banned Freemasonry from her domains – but this does not matter. Far better to take the opera as its original Viennese audiences did – as a sublime pantomime, in which, as in all good fairy tales, right triumphs over evil and all ends happily, with plenty of comic relief along the way.

ACT ONE
SCENE 1 Tamino is lost in a forest, endeavouring to escape from a monstrous serpent. As he falls unconscious, the three ladies appear and kill the serpent with their spears. In an extended trio, they comment on Tamino's beauty, each showing a marked reluctance to leave him alone with either of the others to carry news of his arrival to their mistress, the Queen of Night. They eventually leave together.

Tamino recovers, to hear the sound of pan pipes coming towards him. He hides as a strange-looking individual, half-man, half-bird, enters. It is Papageno, the Queen's bird-catcher – "Der Vogelfänger bin ich ja" ("I am a jolly bird-catcher"). He tells Tamino that he saved him from the serpent but is immediately punished by the returning three ladies for his lie. They secure his mouth with a padlock and then present Tamino with a portrait of the Queen's daughter, Pamina, who, they tell him, is the prisoner of Sarastro, an evil magician. He sings of her beauty – "Dies Bildniss ist bezaubernd schön" ("Oh beautiful beyond compare") – and swears to rescue her from imprisonment. A clap of thunder heralds the approach of the Queen herself, who promises Tamino that Pamina shall be his once she is freed "Oh zittre nicht, mein leiber Sohn" ("Do not be afraid, my beloved son").

Papageno returns, humming piteously, but Tamino, though he would help him if he could, has no power to set him free. The three ladies unlock the padlock and present Tamino with a magic flute and Papageno with a set of magic bells to help them on their way. They also tell them to rely on the guidance of three wise boys.

ACT ONE
SCENE 2 A room in Sarastro's palace. Monostatos is pursuing Pamina, who faints, but, at that moment, Papageno, who has become separated from Tamino, blunders onto the scene. Moor and bird-catcher are equally terrified, but eventually it is Monostatos who flees. Papageno recognizes Pamina as the daughter of the Queen of Night and tells her of Tamino and his love for her, regretting that he himself has found no one to love him. Pamina consoles him and the two sing together – "Bei Männern, welche Liebe fühlen" ("The kindly voice of mother nature") – before going off to search for the prince.

ACT ONE
SCENE 3 A grove outside the temple of Isis and Osiris, which has three entrances, dedicated to Wisdom,

LEFT Tamino with the magic flute, whose powers include the ability to charm wild animals and make them dance.

RIGHT Sarastro proves to be a benevolent high priest, seeking to lead his followers from superstition into enlightenment.

OPPOSITE Pamina comforts Papageno, saying she is sure that he, too, will find someone to love him.

Reason and Nature respectively. The three wise boys, who have led Tamino to the grove, bid him farewell, advising him to be silent, patient and persevering. Tamino approaches the entrances in turn, but, at the first two, stern voices are heard, ordering him back. From the third, however, the Speaker of the temple emerges. He tells Tamino that Sarastro is no tyrant, but a kindly man of wisdom. If Tamino is to become similarly enlightened, he, too, must seek the light. Tamino wonders how he can achieve this goal and is encouraged by an off-stage chorus. Taking up the magic flute, he starts to play and sing, attracting a collection of wild animals who listen and lie at his feet. Suddenly, he hears Papageno's pipes and rushes off to find him.

No sooner has Tamino left the scene than Papageno and Pamina enter from the opposite direction, pursued by Monostatos, who orders his henchmen to bind the two in chains. Papageno, however, takes up his magic bells and sets Moor and henchmen dancing off the stage. The two rejoice in their escape, only to be interrupted by a trumpet call, signalling the approach of Sarastro himself. He enters, greeted by his followers.

Pamina throws herself on Sarastro's mercy, explaining that fear of Monostatos had caused her to flee. Sarastro bids her rise. He is aware of what

has happened and knows that the gods are working to ensure her ultimate happiness. At this moment, Monostatos returns, dragging Tamino with him. As the two lovers recognize each other, the Moor demands that the intruder be punished, but, to his horror, Sarastro orders that Monostatos himself be taken off and soundly beaten. Turning to Tamino and Pamina, he orders them to follow him into the temple, where they will undergo trials to test their love. The chorus hails his wisdom.

ACT TWO SCENE 1 A solemn march sets the scene for Sarastro's address to the temple priests. He tells them that the gods have willed Pamina should marry Tamino, but first the couple must prove they are worthy and enlightened, so thwarting the evil intentions of the Queen of Night. He and the priests pray to Isis and Osiris to give Pamina and Tamino the strength to face their coming ordeals.

ACT TWO SCENE 2 A deep vault within the temple. Tamino and Papageno are warned by two priests that their trials are about to begin, the first involving a vow of silence. No sooner have the priests departed, however, than the three ladies appear and urge the two to

WOLFGANG AMADEUS MOZART

....

Die Zauberflöte

RIGHT As a final test of their worth, Tamino and Pamina must undergo trials by fire and water. They pass safely through both, thanks to their love and the protective powers of the magic flute.

BELOW Before Papageno can hang himself, the Three Boys appear to remind him that although his pipes have failed to attract Papagena, he has forgotten to try his magic bells.

flee with them, but, although Papageno is sorely tempted to speak, Tamino reminds him of the oath they have sworn. Angry off-stage voices are heard and the three ladies flee. The priests congratulate Tamino and Papageno on passing their first test and lead them off to their next trial.

ACT TWO SCENE 3 Pamina is asleep in a bower in the temple garden, observed by Monostatos, who sings of his thwarted passions. As he approaches the slumbering princess, he is startled by a cry of "Zurück!" ("back!") and the appearance of the Queen of Night herself. She wakens her daughter, tells her it is now her task to kill Sarastro and presents her with a dagger with which to perform the deed – "Der Hölle Rache" ("I'll have revenge"). She disappears in another clap of thunder. Monostatos, who has overheard the plot, tries to blackmail the innocent Pamina, but he, in turn, is overheard by Sarastro, who dismisses him from his service. He leaves, promising to try his luck with the Queen.

Pamina pleads with Sarastro to spare her mother. He assures her that he has no intention of exacting vengeance "In diesen heil'gen Hallen" ("Within these holy halls").

ACT TWO SCENE 4 In another hall within the temple and ordered to keep silence again, Tamino and Papageno are alone. Papageno continually chatters to himself, but Tamino remains true to his oath. An old woman enters, and Papageno enters into conversation with her. She is just about to tell him her name when she vanishes in a clap of thunder and is replaced by the three wise boys, bearing wine, food, the magic flute and the magic bells. Tamino picks up the flute and starts to play. The sound brings Pamina to him, but, when Tamino ignores her (Papageno has his mouth full), she despairingly sings of his betrayal – "Ach, ich fühl's" ("Lost for ever").

ACT TWO SCENE 5 The assembled priests sing a chorus of praise to Isis and Osiris, after which Sarastro orders Pamina and Tamino to be brought before him to pay their last farewells to each other.

ACT TWO SCENE 6 Papageno, who has become separated from Tamino in the dark, is wandering miserably around the

underground passages. He is rescued by a priest, who tells him he will never make an initiate but that the gods will grant him one wish. Papageno promptly asks for a goblet of wine, which miraculously appears, but he still feels dissatisfied. Playing his bells, he sings of his desire for "Ein Mädchen, oder Weibchen" ("A girl, or a little wife"), but his pleas are answered by the return of the old woman he had met before. To overcome Papageno's reluctance to swear to be true to her, she tells him that he will be condemned to perpetual imprisonment and a diet of bread and water if he refuses. When he agrees, she casts off her cloak to reveal herself as the young, beautiful feathered Papagena of his dreams. She is promptly hurried off by a priest, pursued by the ardent Papageno.

ACT TWO SCENE 7 The three boys are discovered singing in the garden of the power of the Sun to drive away darkness and fear. Pamina enters, bent on suicide, but, as she raises her mother's dagger, the boys intervene. They explain that Tamino has only been true to his oath, and all four leave together to find him.

ACT TWO SCENE 8 Two priests, standing guard before two doorways, intone a solemn chorale, as Tamino enters for his final test, the ordeal by fire and by water. He is

ABOVE The forces of night defeated, the inhabitants of the temple hail Tamino, **Pamina, Sarastro and the healing power of light.**

joined by Pamina, to whom he is now finally allowed to speak. Protected by their love and the power of the magic flute, they pass successfully through their final trials, their achievement being hailed by a jubilant chorus.

ACT TWO SCENE 9 An orchard. Papageno has lost track of Papagena and is in despair. He tries summoning her with his pipes, to no avail, but, just as he is about to hang himself from a convenient tree, he is saved by the intervention of the three boys, who tell him to try the power of his magic bells. Papagena immediately appears, and the two sing of their forthcoming happiness with a brood of little Papagenae.

ACT TWO SCENE 10 Monostatos, the three ladies and the Queen of Night stealthily enter to launch their attack on the temple, but they are driven away by the powers of light. Sarastro hails Tamino and Pamina as the new guardians of wisdom, and a chorus of rejoicing brings the opera to an end.

Mussorgsky (1839–81)

BORIS GODUNOV

Opera in a prologue and four acts, libretto by the composer after the play by Alexander Pushkin and Nikolai Karamzin's History of the Russian State

Modest Mussorgsky was a leading member of the group of Russian composers known as the Five, who sought to promote an individual Russian musical style. Anticipating later composers, such as Bartók and Kodály, Mussorgsky made substantial use of folk song in his work. In the form he intended it, his orchestration has a uniquely powerful sound all of its own. However, we are still more familiar with Boris Godunov and the symphonic poem A Night on the Bald Mountain in the versions later reorchestrated by his friend Rimsky-Korsakov.

FIRST performed complete (second Mussorgsky version) on 27 January 1874 in St Petersburg; first heard outside Russia in Paris in 1908 (second Rimsky-Korsakov version); first American performance in New York, 1913, under Arturo Toscanini; first British performance in London the same year, with Feodor Chaliapin as Boris.

The performing history of *Boris Godunov* is long and chequered; there are no fewer than four main performing versions, two prepared by Mussorgsky himself and two by Rimsky-Korsakov after the composer's death. The version normally used today is Rimsky-Korsakov's final one, in which he restored cuts he had previously made while retaining his own additions to the reorchestrated score.

PROLOGUE After a short prelude, the curtain rises on the courtyard of a monastery outside Moscow. It is crowded with serfs, who are ordered by a police officer to keep up their prayers for guidance, although it soon becomes clear that they have no idea what they are praying for or why they are there. The prayer is interrupted by Tchelkalov, who announces that Boris has still not yielded to the pleas of the boyars and accepted the vacant throne. A chorus of pilgrims passes across the stage as the curtain falls.

The scene shifts to the courtyard of the Kremlin. Bells are pealing as a stately procession of boyars crosses the stage. Prince Shuisky proclaims Boris as the new tsar and the chorus burst into a song of praise. Boris appears and prays for the guidance of his predecessor in his task. He calls on the boyars to accompany him to pray before the tombs of Russia's past rulers; after this, all shall feast in celebration as his guests. The chorus of acclamation bursts out again as the curtain falls.

CAST

Tchelkalov
clerk of the Duma
Baritone

Prince Shuisky
Tenor

Boris Godunov
tsar of Russia
Bass-baritone

Pimen
an old monk
Bass

Grigory
(later Dmitri, the false pretender)
Tenor

The landlady
of an inn
Mezzo-soprano

Varlaam
a vagabond monk
Bass

Missail
a vagabond monk
Tenor

Nikitch
captain of police
Bass

Fyodor
Boris's son
Mezzo-soprano

Xenia
Boris's daughter
Soprano

Their nurse
Contralto

Marina Mnishek
a Polish princess
Mezzo-soprano

Rangoni
a Jesuit
Bass

The Simpleton
Tenor

Chorus
Boyars, monks, pilgrims, soldiers, Jesuits, Polish nobles, Russian people

RIGHT In the courtyard of the Kremlin, with church bells pealing in the background, the citizens of Moscow assemble to greet their new tsar. In response to Prince Shuisky's cry "Long live Tsar Boris Feodorvitch", they burst into a chorus of rejoicing.

ACT ONE
SCENE 1

Five years have passed and Russia faces famine, plague and rebellion, for all of which Boris is blamed. The curtain rises on a monk's cell. It is late at night and Pimen is labouring over the Russian history he is writing. The sound of off-stage chanting awakens Grigory, Pimen's young companion. He tells Pimen that he has had a strange dream: he stood at the top of a high tower in Moscow, being mocked by the people, eventually falling only to awaken. Pimen tries to comfort him, but Grigory is not to be consoled. Finally, he asks Pimen how old Dmitri, the brother of Boris's predecessor as tsar, would have been had he not been murdered and Pimen replies that he would have been about as old as Grigory himself. He leaves for Matins, but Grigory lingers behind, swearing that Boris shall not escape the judgement of heaven for his crimes.

ACT ONE
SCENE 2

An inn on the Lithuanian border. The landlady sings a happy nonsense song, but she is interrupted by two ruffianly monks, Varlaam and Missail. They are accompanied by Grigory, who is fleeing to Lithuania, pursued by the tsar's police. Varlaam launches into a boastful song about his achievements at the battle of Kazan; while he sings, Grigory asks the landlady the safest way to reach Lithuania.

RIGHT Boris appears before his people. Faced with the responsibilities of his position, he pauses before leading the boyars into the cathedral to pray for the strength to guide Russia.

55

MODEST PETROVICH MUSSORGSKY

. . . .

Boris Godunov

LEFT **In the first of his great monologues, Boris reveals his troubled conscience. The ghost of the murdered tsarevich seems to rise from the grave to haunt him.**

The police suddenly burst into the room. They are looking for Grigory, but their captain cannot read and so hands the description he has been given to Grigory himself to read aloud. This he does, substituting a description of Varlaam for that of himself. Varlaam snatches the paper and laboriously starts to spell it out, word by word. As it becomes clear that Grigory is the wanted man, he jumps through the inn window and escapes.

ACT TWO In the royal apartments in the Kremlin, Fyodor sits reading while his sister sings sadly. Their nurse tries to comfort her and then sings a nursery song. There follows a clapping game, in which all three join, but this is interrupted by Boris's entrance. In the first of his great monologues, "I have attained the highest power", he pours out his woes to Fyodor, including the remorse he feels when he thinks of the murdered Dmitri.

Prince Shuisky is announced. Boris denounces him for his double-dealing with the Poles, who are invading Russia, and treacherous rebels, but Shuisky quickly counters with the announcement that a pretender, calling himself Dmitri, is on the march, supported by the king of Poland. At the mention of Dmitri's name, Boris, dismissing his son, starts to confer anxiously with Shuisky. The latter tells the tsar he can indeed confirm the facts of Dmitri's death, but, as he relates them, Boris who can bear no more, orders him out of the room. He feels he is suffocating and, as a clock starts to chime, has a hallucination, in which the murdered Dmitri appears. He sinks to the ground, praying for God to forgive him.

ACT THREE
SCENE 1 Marina's apartments. She sings of her ambitions and her aim, by marrying Dmitri, of ascending the Russian throne. Rangoni, a Jesuit, appears. He orders Marina to remember her Catholic faith and that it is her duty to turn the Russians away from the Orthodox Church.

ACT THREE
SCENE 2 The scene shifts to a moonlit garden. Grigory enters, richly dressed, having assumed the role of pretender. He sings of his love for Marina; as he impatiently awaits her arrival, her love is confirmed by Rangoni, who slips into the shadows as Marina and her court enter. The nobles dance a lively polonaise, after which Grigory and Marina are

left on their own. She spurs him on to lead his army on Moscow, and the two sing of their new-found love. As they embrace, Rangoni can be seen looking on approvingly.

ACT FOUR
SCENE 1
The Duma is in session, debating on what steps to take to suppress the rebellion. Shuisky enters and tells them of Boris's hallucinations of a murdered child, to be closely followed by the tsar himself, in a state of near collapse. A monk, who, Shuisky says, is the bearer of important news, is given permission to enter. It is Pimen, who tells of a miracle that has taken place at Dmitri's tomb.

Boris falls into the arms of his boyars. He knows that he is dying and sends for Fyodor. Father and son are left alone. Boris bids farewell to him and tells him to uphold his place as rightful tsar. The boyars re-enter and as they, and off-stage monks, pray for Boris's soul, he dies.

ACT FOUR
SCENE 2
A clearing in the forest of Krony. The rebels are on the march and the crowd bait a boyar they have captured. A simpleton sings a sad little song, but a group of children run off with the few kopeks he has managed to collect. Varlaam and Missail sing the praises of the pretender; when two Jesuits enter, they denounce them to the crowd, which prepares to lynch them.

Grigory enters with his troops. He orders the release of boyar and Jesuits and summons the people to follow him to Moscow. The stage clears and the simpleton is discovered sitting alone. The curtain falls on his lament for the sufferings of the Russian people.

(Mussorgsky wrote this scene to replace another one, which was originally placed at the start of the act, before the death of Boris. Outside St Basil's Cathedral in Moscow, the simpleton turns to Boris, as he leaves the service, and asks him to punish the children who have robbed him, just as Boris punished Dmitri. Boris asks the simpleton to pray for him, but the latter refuses, saying no one can pray for a Herod. Many modern productions include both scenes.)

LEFT **Dmitri, the pretender to the throne who is in reality the monk Grigory, has made his way to the Polish court. There he falls in love with Princess Marina. She urges him to march on Moscow. If he is not prepared to crown her as his tsarina, he cannot really love her.**

BELOW **A poor simpleton and the guilt-ridden tsar confront each other on the steps of St Basil's Cathedral. The simpleton appeals to Boris to punish the children who have robbed him of a few kopeks, but when Boris offers him money, he refuses to take gold from the hands of a murderer.**

Puccini (1858–1924)

LA BOHÈME

Opera in four acts, text by Giuseppe Giacosa and Luigi Illica, based on the novel by Henri Murger

Giacomo Puccini had his first major success with Manon Lescaut in 1893. He subsequently wrote 11 more operas, of which La Bohème, Tosca, Madama Butterfly and Turandot are a staple part of the repertory of every major international opera house. He was helped in his rise by the patronage and encouragement of the great music publisher Ricordi; his operas are notable for the sheer romantic beauty of their melodies and for their theatrical cunning.

*L*A *Bohème (The Bohemians)* was first performed at the Teatro Regio, Turin, on 1 February 1896. Its first British performance was in Manchester in 1897; the American première was staged in Los Angeles the same year.

With *La Bohème*, the first performance of which was conducted by the young Arturo Toscanini, Puccini established his dominance of the Italian operatic stage. The opera has remained at the core of the repertory ever since.

ACT ONE A garret high in the Latin Quarter of Paris on Christmas Eve. Rodolfo is writing and Marcello painting, both complaining of the cold. Rodolfo decides to sacrifice his new play to feed their stove and, joined by Colline, the three try to warm themselves as the play is all too quickly consumed. Colline and Marcello boo the author and a playful scuffle develops. This is interrupted by the entrance of Schaunard, who tosses money to the floor and is followed by errand boys carrying baskets of food and drink. As his friends fall on the provisions, he tells them of an eccentric Englishman who employed him to play to silence a parrot. He eventually succeeded by secretly poisoning the bird with a drop of arsenic.

To celebrate Christmas, the Bohemians decide to go out for a meal at the nearby Café Momus, but their landlord, Benoit, comes knocking at the door for his rent. Plying him with wine, they lead him on to describe his female conquests, whereupon they feign indignation at his immorality and throw him out, without his rent. Rodolfo tells his friends that he will join them later – he has an article to write for a magazine – and they leave, urging him to hurry.

Rodolfo starts to write but quickly throws down his pen. There is a timid knock at the door, and a woman's voice is heard. It is his neighbour, Mimi,

Marcello
a painter
Baritone

Rodolfo
a poet
Tenor

Colline
a philosopher
Bass

Schaunard
a musician
Baritone

Benoit
their landlord
Bass

Mimi
a seamstress
Soprano

Musetta
a grisette
Soprano

Parpignol
a toy seller
Tenor

Alcindoro
Musetta's admirer
Bass

Customs sergeant
Bass

Chorus
Parisians, students, customs officers, soldiers, children

LEFT Rodolfo declares his love for the seamstress Mimi, hailing her beauty as it is captured in the moonlight streaming in through his studio window.

whose candle has gone out on the stairs and who is looking for a light. As Rodolfo obliges her, she is racked by a sudden coughing fit and he sits her down in a chair. Both candles are now extinguished – Mimi's by a gust of wind, while Rodolfo slyly puts his out – and they search for her door key, which she has dropped on the floor by moonlight. Rodolfo finds the key and quickly pockets it. Their two hands meet.

There follows the most celebrated tenor aria Puccini ever wrote – "Che gelida manina" ("Your tiny hand is frozen") – in which Rodolfo explains who he is and what he dreams. Mimi, in turn, sings her story – "Mi chiamo Mimi" ("My name is Mimi"). Rodolfo's impatient friends return and

call up from the street. Mimi moves to the window and is revealed in the moonlight. Rodolfo exclaims "O soave fanciulla" ("Vision of loveliness"), and the two begin a flowing, lyrical love duet, which ends off-stage, as they make their way down the stairs and to the café.

ACT TWO In a square in front of the Café Momus shoppers are bustling about on all sides, street sellers are peddling their wares, and harassed waiters are setting out tables outside the café itself. Rodolfo buys Mimi a new bonnet before introducing her to his friends, who have taken one of the outside tables.

La Bohème

LEFT **Outside the Café Momus, Musetta, Marcello's former lover, sings a teasing waltz to attract his attention. She sends her elderly admirer, Alcindoro, away to get her shoes mended, and she and Marcello fall into each other's arms.**

Parpignol, a toy seller, crosses the scene, pursued by a band of children whose mothers vainly try to restrain them. Food and drink is ordered, but the happy party is interrupted by the arrival of the flighty Musetta, Marcello's former lover who has taken up with the rich, but old, Alcindoro. Marcello pretends to ignore her and, in an effort to capture his attention, she sings the catchy waltz song "Quando me'n vo soletta per la via" ("As I make my way through the street"). As her song rises to a climax, she suddenly complains to Alcindoro that her shoe is pinching, and, as Marcello takes up the refrain, she sends Alcindoro off to a cobbler.

The reunited lovers embrace, and Musetta joins the Bohemians at their table. The waiter brings the bill, but Schaunard seems to have spent all his money. Musetta is equal to the situation – the gentleman who was with her will pay! As the night patrol, headed by its drum-major, crosses the stage, the Bohemians run off behind it. The crowd mocks Alcindoro, who has just returned from the cobbler's to find no Musetta but an enormous bill.

ACT THREE At a gateway to the city, off the Rue d'Enfer, the sound of carousing voices comes from an inn, while, beyond the gate, early morning workers and peasants are waiting to be admitted to the city. Eventually, the sleepy customs officers raise their barrier and the crowd disperses. Mimi, racked by her cough, enters and asks a woman passer-by if she knows the whereabouts of Marcello. The woman offers to go into the inn to fetch him, and as she does so, Mimi is again stricken by her vicious cough.

Marcello, who is living at the inn with Musetta, enters. He greets Mimi and asks her to come into the warm, but, learning that Rodolfo is inside, she bursts into tears, telling him that Rodolfo is so jealous of her it is better that they part. Hearing

RIGHT **Mimi explains to Marcello that Rodolfo's jealousy makes it impossible for their affair to continue and that the time has come for them to part.**

LEFT Rodolfo tells Marcello that Mimi makes him so jealous with her heartless behaviour that he has resolved to leave her.

BELOW The exhausted Mimi falls asleep, a sleep from which she will never awaken. She dies of cold and consumption, but happy that she and Rodolfo have been reconciled.

Rodolfo approach, she conceals herself while he tells Marcello his side of the story – Mimi is heartless and he wants to give her up because they are always quarrelling. Another coughing fit gives Mimi away, and the two sing sadly together of their mutual decision. Marcello, meanwhile, has caught Musetta flirting in the tavern, and what was a duet becomes a quartet as both sets of lovers part.

ACT FOUR   Back in the attic, both Rodolfo and Marcello are pining for their former loves. With Colline and Schaunard they improvise a mock feast with a bloater and water bottle and then fight a mock duel. The horseplay is at its height when Musetta bursts in; Mimi, who is with her, is dying and, as a last request, has asked to return to the attic where she was once so happy. Rodolfo gently carries her to the bed and takes her hands in his. Musetta gives her earrings to Marcello, who goes off to pawn them and buy medicine, Colline following to do the same with his overcoat.

Mimi and Rodolfo remind one another of their early love until she says she is tired and wants to sleep. Suddenly, the others realize that she is dead. Rodolfo reads what has happened in their tragic faces and hurls himself on her. His sobs rise as the curtain falls.

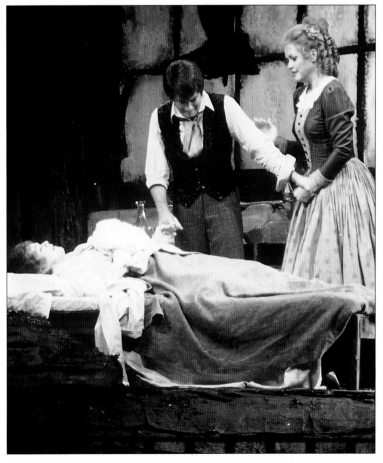

TOSCA

Opera in three acts, libretto by Giuseppe Giacosa and Luigi Illica, based on the play by Victorien Sardou

CAST

Angelotti
a political prisoner
Bass

The Sacristan
Baritone

Mario Cavaradossi
a painter
Tenor

Floria Tosca
a famous singer
Soprano

Baron Scarpia
chief of police
Baritone

Spoletta
a police agent
Tenor

Sciarrone
another police agent
Bass

A shepherd boy
Alto

A gaoler
Bass

Chorus
Choristers, police
agents, soldiers,
citizens of Rome

LEFT Tosca jealously accuses her lover Cavaradossi of preferring another woman. He denies that there is anyone else, and the two sing of their love.

LEFT The evil Baron
Scarpia declares that
his obsession with
Tosca would make him
forget God – and
immediately leads the
congregation in the *Te
Deum* celebrating the
supposed defeat of
Napleon at Marengo.

Tosca was first performed at the Teatro Constanzi, Rome, on 14 January 1900; its first British performance was in London at the Royal Opera House, Covent Garden later the same year. Its first American performance was at the Metropolitan Opera, New York, in 1901.

Although condemned by some as a "shabby little shocker", Puccini's *Tosca* can still be a gripping theatrical experience, especially when great singing actors are involved. When Maria Callas and Tito Gobbi sang the roles of Tosca and Scarpia at the Royal Opera House, for instance, their combined stage genius made the second act a totally unforgettable theatrical experience. Another memorable *Tosca* was the live staging in the actual Roman locations specified by Puccini, which was televised world-wide in the summer of 1992.

ACT ONE Three sinister chords, played *fff tutta forza* by the full orchestra and depicting Scarpia, precede the rise of the curtain on the church of Sant' Andrea della Valle, Rome. The fleeing Angelotti, a former consul of the Roman Republic, enters. He has escaped from the castle of Sant' Angelo and is seeking refuge. His sister, the Marchese Attavanti, has hidden the key of the family chapel at the foot of the statue of the Madonna, and as footsteps are heard approaching, Angelotti finds the key, and gets into the chapel.

Enter the Sacristan, who busies himself dusting and cleaning. The angelus sounds and he kneels in prayer. Cavaradossi now enters. He examines the portrait of Mary Magdalene he has been painting and admits to himself that it has been inspired by two women, Tosca, his lover, and the Marchese. The Sacristan goes out, and Angelotti emerges from his hiding place. Cavaradossi recognizes him and agrees to help him escape. At that moment, Tosca's voice is heard off-stage calling to Cavaradossi. The painter thrusts a basket of food lying at the foot of his easel into Angelotti's hands and hurries him back into hiding.

Tosca sweeps into the church. She has overheard Cavaradossi whispering, and her natural jealousy convinces her he has been talking with a secret lover. Eventually he manages to reassure her, and they arrange to meet that evening after she has finished her performance and steal away to Cavaradossi's country villa. He urges her to leave so that he can continue with his painting, but this reawakens her suspicions, especially when she, too, recognizes the features of the Marchese in the portrait. Cavaradossi counters by asking her whose eyes could be more beautiful than her own.

Tosca

LEFT Jealous she may be, but, underneath it all, Tosca is totally devoted to Cavaradossi. Here she assures him that, despite Scarpia's threats and witnessing his torture, she has not betrayed Angelotti's hiding place.

Tosca leaves and Cavardossi releases Angelotti. They are talking in whispers of the hated Scarpia when they hear a cannon shot signifying that Angelotti's escape has been discovered. Cavaradossi offers to hide him in a disused well in the grounds of his villa, and the two run off together.

The Sacristan bustles in with the news (later proved false) that the Austrians have defeated Napoleon at Marengo and that Tosca will be the soloist in a thanksgiving cantata to be sung that evening at the Palazzo Farnese. As the choirboys dance around and the Sacristan vainly tries to keep order, Scarpia, accompanied by Spoletta, who has traced Angelotti to the church, enters and the hubbub ceases.

Scarpia orders the church to be searched, and the search reveals not only the empty food basket but also a fan, decorated with the Attavanti coat of arms. It is clear to Scarpia that the painter has connived in Angelotti's escape. Tosca returns to tell her lover that she will not now be able to meet him as arranged, only to find Scarpia instead. He himself lusts after the singer and reawakens her jealousy by showing her the fan, suggesting it is evidence of an assignation between Cavaradossi and the Marchese. As she storms out, he tells

Spoletta to follow her in the belief that she will lead them to Cavaradossi and, he hopes, Angelotti as well.

As a celebratory *Te Deum* begins, Scarpia exults in his power to be able to send Cavaradossi to the firing squad and to possess Tosca – for her, he would renounce God. He kneels and joins in the *Te Deum*.

ACT TWO Scarpia is dining alone in his rooms in the Palazzo Farnese, anticipating his conquest of Tosca, to whom he sends a note, asking her to come to him after her performance. Spoletta returns. He has not succeeded in recapturing Angelotti but has Cavaradossi under guard. As Scarpia starts to interrogate the painter, Tosca's voice is heard leading the cantata. Failing to get any information out of Cavaradossi, Scarpia orders him to be taken to the torture chamber, just as Tosca arrives. Before he is dragged away, her lover warns her, under his breath, to keep silent.

Tosca is left alone with Scarpia to face his questions. When she, too, fails to give him the information he seeks, he orders a concealed door to be opened, so that she can hear her lover's cries of anguish. Unable to bear this, she finally reveals

Angelotti's hiding place.

Scarpia orders the torment to cease and Cavaradossi is carried in. As Tosca comforts him, he asks her whether she has given anything away. She is reassuring him when Scarpia exultantly orders Spoletta to hurry to the well in the garden and apprehend Angelotti. Furiously, Cavaradossi turns on Tosca, but, at that moment, Sciarrone, another of Scarpia's agents, rushes in to say the news from Marengo was false – Napoleon has turned defeat into victory and the Austrians are in full retreat. Cavaradossi cries out in jubilation and Scarpia orders his immediate removal and execution.

Alone with Scarpia again, Tosca desperately bargains for her lover's life. Scarpia tells her his price – her body for Cavaradossi's freedom. She agrees and Scarpia orders Spoletta to arrange a mock execution, "Just like the one that was arranged for Palmieri", after which the two lovers will be free to escape. As he writes a safe conduct for them, Tosca catches sight of a sharp knife on the supper table. When Scarpia moves to embrace her, she snatches it up and stabs him. He falls dying. Trembling, she prises the safe conduct from his hands. Placing a crucifix on Scarpia's lips and a candle on either side of his corpse, she slips from the room as a drum roll sounds.

ACT THREE The battlements of the Castel Sant' Angelo. It is just before dawn. Sheep bells sound in the distance and a shepherd boy is heard singing. The bells of the city strike the hour and Cavaradossi is led in. He bribes his gaoler to allow him to write a last farewell to Tosca.

No sooner has he finished than Tosca herself arrives with the safe conduct, and she tells him that she has murdered Scarpia. The two lovers sing of their future and rehearse the mock execution together. Spoletta and the firing squad enter, the salvo is fired and Cavaradossi falls. "Look how well he acts it," exclaims Tosca, as the soldiers file off. She urges him to rise, but there is no response. As she approaches the body, she realizes that Scarpia has tricked her and that this is no fake execution but grim reality.

Distant shouts are heard – Scarpia's corpse has been discovered. As Spoletta hastens onto the scene to arrest her, Tosca, with the cry "Scarpia, we shall meet before God", leaps from the battlements to meet her death on the rocks below.

LEFT Tosca sings movingly that she has lived her life solely for her art and for love. Now she is being compelled to yield to Scarpia's demands in order to save Cavaradossi from the firing squad.

ABOVE Tosca has killed Scarpia, but she has been tricked. The mock execution that she thought Scarpia had arranged turned out to be real. As Scarpia's minions arrive to arrest her, she hurls herself to her death, crying "Scarpia, we shall meet before God".

MADAMA BUTTERFLY

Opera in three acts, libretto by Giuseppe Giacosa and Luigi Illica, based on the play by David Belasco

CAST

B. F. Pinkerton
Lieutenant, US Navy
Tenor

Goro
a marriage broker
Tenor

Sharpless
US consul at
Nagasaki
Baritone

Cio-Cio-San
Madame Butterfly
Soprano

Suzuki
her maid
Mezzo-soprano

**The Imperial
Commissioner**
Bass

**The Official
Registrar**
Baritone

The Bonze
Butterfly's uncle
Bass

Prince Yamadori
Baritone

Trouble
Butterfly's baby son
—

Kate Pinkerton
Soprano

Chorus
Japanese friends
and relatives

LEFT Resplendent in full dress uniform, Pinkerton pledges his love to Butterfly.

MADAMA *Butterfly (Madame Butterfly)* was first performed at La Scala, Milan, on 17 February 1904; the revised version received its première at Brescia in May. The first British performance was in London in 1905 at the Royal Opera House, Covent Garden; the first American staging was at Washington (in English) the following year.

The first performance of what is one of the world's most popular operas was a fiasco; the La Scala audience, it is thought, objected to the resemblance between the theme used for Butterfly's entrance and that of Mimi's first entrance in *La Bohème* and also to the length of the second act (the original *Butterfly* had only two acts, as opposed to the revised version's three). Even after the latter triumphed at Brescia, Puccini continued his revisions; the final version, and the one normally played today, dates from December 1906 and was prepared for the French première at the Opéra-Comique, Paris.

ACT ONE A prelude, based on a Japanese tune, sets the mood for the whole of the first act, into which the prelude leads without a break. Pinkerton is on the point of contracting a Japanese marriage with Butterfly, and, as the curtain rises, he is with Goro the marriage broker, looking over the house he has rented for her. Sharpless, who disapproves of Pinkerton's plan, arrives and makes a last attempt to dissuade him. It may be a passing whim for the young lieutenant, but for a Japanese girl it may be deadly serious. Pinkerton laughs off these fears and drinks to his future American bride.

Further discussion is interrupted by the arrival of Butterfly with her friends and relatives. Sharpless's fears are quickly confirmed: Butterfly does not regard this a marriage of convenience, as her husband-to-be does. She has even gone as far as secretly changing her religion to prepare herself for her new life. As the marriage contract is signed and the celebrations start, the Bonze, Butterfly's uncle, arrives on the scene. He has discovered her change of faith and curses her, calling on the relatives to renounce her. The furious Pinkerton drives them from the house. Butterfly is weeping, but Pinkerton comforts her in the long love duet that ends the act.

ACT TWO Three years have passed. Pinkerton has sailed away, promising to return to Butterfly, who, in the meantime, has given birth to his child. Suzuki, convinced that her mistress has been deserted, nevertheless prays for Pinkerton's safe return. Butterfly is confident that this will not be long delayed, and she paints a vivid picture of what the home-coming will be like in the aria "Un bel dì vedremo" ("One fine day").

Sharpless comes in with news for Butterfly. Pinkerton is indeed on his way back to Nagasaki but accompanied by his American wife, Kate. Butterfly, however, is so overcome by the fact that Pinkerton has written a letter that Sharpless cannot make the situation clear. He tries again, but is interrupted by Goro, who is accompanied by Yamadori, a wealthy Japanese prince, whom Goro urges Butterfly to marry. The money Pinkerton left her is spent and poverty stares her in the face. Butterfly indignantly rejects the proposal.

Sharpless makes a third and final attempt to open Butterfly's eyes to the truth, but her answer is to bring in her baby son. Once Pinkerton knows what a fine child he has he is sure to return. What would she do if he did not return, asks Sharpless. Butterfly explains that she would then have two choices – to return to her old life as a geisha or to die.

A cannon shot from the harbour announces a ship's arrival. It is Pinkerton's ship, the *Abraham Lincoln*. Excitedly, Butterfly and Suzuki decorate the house with cherry blossom for Pinkerton's return. As night falls, she, Suzuki and the baby peer out through three holes Butterfly has pierced in the paper wall, looking out for Pinkerton's approach.

ACT THREE Dawn is breaking. Suzuki and the baby are fast asleep, but Butterfly is still watching and waiting. Suzuki wakens and persuades her to go and rest. Sharpless and Pinkerton appear, Pinkerton accompanied by his new bride. Seeing the proof of Butterfly's devotion, he rushes off in remorse, leaving Sharpless to settle matters as best he can.

Butterfly re-enters, expecting to see Pinkerton, but eventually has to face the truth. She tells Kate that, if Pinkerton will return in half an hour, he can take his son. The two withdraw. Butterfly bids farewell to the child and, as Pinkerton returns, stabs herself to death with her father's ceremonial sword.

LEFT Sharpless tries to break the news to Butterfly that, although Pinkerton is returning to Nagasaki, he is bringing with him his new American wife.

TURANDOT

Opera in three acts, libretto by Giuseppe Adami and Renato Simoni, based on the play by Carlo Gozzi

CAST

A mandarin
Baritone

Timur
exiled ruler of Tartary
Bass

Liù
a slave girl
Soprano

Calaf
Timur's son
Tenor

Turandot
princess of China
Soprano

Prince of Persia
Tenor

Ping, Pang and Pong
imperial ministers
Baritone, tenor, tenor

Altoun
emperor of China
Tenor

Chorus
Courtiers, soldiers,
citizens of Peking

*T*URANDOT was first performed at La Scala, Milan, on 25 April 1926 and first performed in America at the Metropolitan Opera, New York, in the autumn of the same year. The first British performance was at the Royal Opera House, Covent Garden, London, in May 1927.

Puccini left *Turandot* unfinished at his death; Arturo Toscanini ended the first performance after the mournful miniature march that follows the death of Liù in Act 3, turning to the audience with the words "Here the master laid down his pen". The opera was completed by Puccini's pupil, Franco Alfano, who had access to the sketches that his master had made for the duet of reconciliation between Calaf and Turandot and for the final scene, but Toscanini did not like the Alfano completion and cut it when he came to perform it. This is the version normally heard today, which, to a great extent, explains the truncated nature of the final scenes.

ACT ONE As the curtain rises, the Peking mob is awaiting the result of the latest trial in the imperial palace. The Prince of Persia is the most recent suitor for the hand of Princess Turandot; he must correctly answer the three riddles she has set, or pay for failure with his head. A mandarin announces that the Prince has failed the test, and the crowd urge the headsman and his assistants to sharpen the ceremonial execution sword. Mingling with the crowd are Timur and Liù, his faithful slave. By accident, they meet Calaf, Timur's son, whom he had thought dead. Their joyful reunion is overshadowed by fear of the plotters who have usurped Timur's throne. He tells of his flight, which was aided only by Liù; when Calaf asks her why she, a slave, risked her life for his father, she answers because he once smiled at her.

The moon rises, the signal for the execution to take place. As the failed Prince leads a procession through the crowd, the mood changes and voices are heard calling for mercy, while Calaf curses the person responsible. Turandot brifly appears and signals for the execution to proceed, but the brief glimpse he has caught of her is enough for Calaf to fall madly in love with her. Liù and Timur plead with him to desist, their arguments being supported by the three imperial ministers who now enter. Calaf assures them he will be victorious and, as the curtain falls, he sounds the great gong to signal that a new challenger for Turandot's hand has emerged.

ACT TWO Ping, Pang and Pong lament the sad state of China. Drums are heard in the distance, and they withdraw, while, to the strains of a majestic march, the scene changes to the imperial throne room, where Calaf's trial is to take place. The aged Altoun begs Calaf to withdraw – too many have already perished – but he is determined to proceed. Turandot tells the story of her ancestress, who was betrayed by a foreign conqueror and carried into exile, where she died of grief. It is to avenge her that Turandot has devised her test.

Turandot asks her first riddle, which Calaf quickly solves. He succeeds with the second, though more slowly, but hesitates over the third – "What is the ice that sets men on fire?" Turandot taunts Calaf that death is near, but suddenly he guesses the answer. It is Turandot herself.

The princess begs her father not to force her into marriage, but he replies that the unknown prince has won her fairly and she must abide by the rules she herself set. Calaf chivalrously intercedes. He will set her the task of discovering his name by morning. If she fails, she is his, but, if she succeeds, he will forfeit his life.

ABOVE **Turandot recounts the story of her ancestress, the Princess Lou Ling, whose grim fate she has determined to avenge by setting her suitors three impossible riddles to solve. Failure means death.**

LEFT **Tortured to make her reveal Calaf's name, Liù snatches a dagger from one of the guards and stabs herself rather than betray her master.**

ACT THREE In the gardens of the palace the mandarin's voice is heard proclaiming Turandot's latest decree: no one shall sleep until the stranger's name is discovered. Calaf is unmoved, convinced that he will succeed and claim Turandot as his bride. In the aria "Nessun dorma" ("None shall sleep") he sings of his coming victory. Ping, Pang and Pong try bribes and then threats to find out the secret. Turandot's guards enter with Timur and Liù. Turandot orders Timur to be tortured to force him to reveal the name, but Liù steps forward. Such torture is useless, for only she knows the true identity of the unknown prince. She is tortured until she can bear it no more. Telling Turandot that it is love that has given her the power to resist, she snatches a dagger from a guard and stabs herself to death. The grieving Timur and the crowd bear her body away. Calaf turns on Turandot for her cruelty and then kisses her on the mouth. The kiss breaks her resistance and she submits. Calaf, knowing he has won his gamble, tells her his name. Trumpets sound and the scene switches back to the throne room. Turandot announces she has discovered the stranger's secret. His name is – love. The opera ends in a chorus of rejoicing.

Rossini (1792–1868)

IL BARBIERE DI SIVIGLIA

Opera in two acts, libretto by Cesare Sterbini, after the play by Pierre Beaumarchais

Gioacchino Rossini had the opera in his blood – his father was a trumpet-player and his mother an opera singer. He wrote 36 highly successful operas for the Italian and French stages between 1810 and 1829, when his last – and grandest – work, Guillieme Tell (William Tell) was premiered in Paris. After that he gave up serious composition, with the exception of a mass and a group of pieces called Sins of My Old Age.

I*L Barbiere di Siviglia (The Barber of Seville)* was first performed on 20 February 1816 at the Teatro Argentina, Rome, as *Almaviva: ossia l'Innutile Precauzione (Almaviva: The Useless Precaution)*. The first British performance was at the Haymarket Theatre, London, in 1818; the first American staging was in New York (in English) the following year.

The first night of what was to be retitled *Il Barbiere di Siviglia* was one of the operatic world's great fiascos. Many reasons have been given for this – the Roman public, it is said, had fond memories of the previous opera on the subject by Giovanni Paisiello (the reason the prudent Rossini had changed the title), while a chapter of on-stage accidents did little to pacify the already hostile audience. The second performance, however, was a great success.

In *Il Barbiere*, Rossini's habit of borrowing from himself is fully in evidence. Almaviva's first aria, introduced at the second performance, was bodily lifted from an earlier opera *Aureliano in Palmira* (it had also featured in a cantata, *Ciro in Babilonia*). The overture, too, was borrowed – it had previously been the overture to *Elisabetta, Regina d'Inghilterra*.

ACT ONE
SCENE 1 Outside Dr Bartolo's house in Seville, a band of musicians, superintended by Fiorello, is getting into position. The Count, who is in love with Bartolo's ward, Rosina, has employed them to serenade her. He himself appears and launches into the aria "Ecco ridente in cielo" ("Smiling in the heavens"). There is no sign or sound from the house, so he disconsolately pays off the musicians, but his generosity provokes a noisy chorus of thanks, which he and Fiorello try their best to calm.

A voice is heard off-stage. It is Figaro, the city

CAST

Fiorello
Count Almaviva's servant
Bass

Count Almaviva
Tenor

Figaro
a barber
Baritone

Rosina
Dr Bartolo's ward
Mezzo-soprano

Dr Bartolo
Bass

Don Basilio
a singing teacher
Bass

Bertha
Rosina's governess
Mezzo-soprano

Chorus
Servants, members of the city watch

RIGHT Counting the gold the Count has given him, Figaro tells Almaviva that nothing is more guaranteed to make his scheming brain work its hardest.

barber, who enters and introduces himself in his famous aria "Largo al factotum della città" ("Make way for the city's factotum"). He recognizes the Count as an old friend and immediately agrees to help him arrange a meeting with Rosina, although they will·have to overcome the suspicious Dr Bartolo, who, in league with Don Basilio, Rosina's singing teacher, is plotting to marry his ward himself.

At that moment, a window opens and a note flutters down to the street. It is from Rosina, addressed to her unknown admirer and asking him to tell her his name. As a test of her affections, the Count replies that he is Lindoro, a poor but devoted student. Rosina starts to reply, but her answer is cut short, presumably by the appearance of Dr Bartolo in her room. Inflamed by passion, the Count presses money on Figaro, who tells him there is nothing he cannot accomplish.

ACT ONE
SCENE 2 Inside the house Rosina is discovered singing of the pleasing voice she has just heard – "Una voce poca

fa" ("A little voice I heard just now"). In a brilliant cabaletta, she assures us that although she is mild and docile, she always gets her own way in the end. As she leaves, Bartolo and Don Basilio enter. The doctor tells his friend that he suspects that the Count is in the city and that he is, moreover, his rival for Rosina's affections. What can he do? "Nothing easier" replies Basilio, "simply start a slander – "la calunnia" – about the Count," and goes on to explain just how this can be done. The two go off to scheme.

Figaro enters in search of Bartolo, whom he has come to shave, and takes advantage of Rosina's re-entry to tell her that his "cousin", Lindoro, is madly in love with her. She promptly hands him another note to take to the Count, which she has already written. In a duet she feigns surprise and humility, while Figaro comments on female cleverness. Bartolo returns to tax Rosina with having dropped a note from the balcony. Despite her protestations of innocence, he tells her it is useless to try to deceive him. However, Figaro and the Count are now ready to put the first stage of their

LEFT The cast is frozen into immobility, "just like statues", as the finale to the first act heads towards its climax.

RIGHT Figaro starts on Dr Bartolo's long-delayed shave, but the process is soon interrupted when Bartolo overhears the disguised Count's whispered conversation with Rosina, and promptly turns the supposed singing teacher and barber out of the house in a fury.

plan into action. Almaviva enters, disguised as a drunken soldier, with an order billeting him in the house. Bartolo protests that he has a certificate of exemption, but the Count simply tears it up. Rosina complains of maltreatment, at which the Count takes her side and threatens Bartolo with his sword, despite Figaro's warnings not to over-play his hand for the noise they are making can be heard across Seville.

The city watch enters to find out what is caus-ing the disturbance. Their leader arrests Almaviva, who takes him aside and reveals his true identity. He is promptly released. The assembled company is stunned into silence – "Fredda ed immobile" ("Awestruck and immovable") – but then falls to wrangling again in an irresistible buffa finale.

ACT TWO Dr Bartolo is musing on the events **SCENE 1** of the day when the Count is ad-mitted, this time disguised as a music teacher whom Don Basilio has sent to give Rosina her singing lesson in his place, the Count claiming that Basilio has been taken ill. He worms his way into Bartolo's confidence by producing Rosina's note and saying he will tell her that it was given to him by a mistress of the Count. Rosina enters for her singing lesson, but the song she chooses – an aria from *L'Innutile Precauzione* – is not at all to Bartolo's taste and he, in turn, sings an aria in the style that was popular in his youth.

Figaro arrives to give Bartolo his long-delayed shave, but, at that moment, an unwelcome visitor is announced. It is Basilio, but, helped by the purse of gold the Count slips into his hand, he is quickly persuaded that he is really ill and retires to go home to bed. While Figaro starts shaving Bartolo, the Count and Rosina start to plot their elopement, but, just as he is about to tell her how he has won her guardian's confidence, Bartolo overhears their conversation. In a fury, he drives Almaviva and Figaro out of the house and then shows Rosina the letter. Furious in her turn, she agrees, after all, to marry him. Berta enters, complaining about the topsy-turvy household in which she has the mis-fortune to be employed (this aria is often cut in modern performances).

ACT TWO A storm interlude leads to the final **SCENE 2** scene. Almaviva and Figaro enter with a ladder (an elaborate aria here for the Count is usually omitted), but Rosina refuses to descend until the Count reveals the whole plot and his true identity. The reconciled couple sing breathlessly of their love, while Figaro vainly urges haste. The opportune arrival of a not-ary, whom Bartolo has engaged, means that the two can be formally betrothed and, when Bartolo comes on the scene, he is told that he is too late and his plot has failed. The opera ends in general reconciliation.

DIE FLEDERMAUS

Opera in three acts, libretto by Karl Haffner and Richard Genée after the French comedy Le Réveillon *by Henri Meilhac and Ludovic Halévy*

Johann Strauss succeeded his father as Vienna's "waltz king", founding his own orchestra at the age of 18. His best-known waltz is** The Blue Danube**, which has become the unofficial second National Anthem of Austria. In addition to** Die Fledermaus**, he wrote 16 other operettas, the best-known of which are** The Gypsy Baron **and** A Night in Venice**. However, his attempts at grand opera were a complete failure.

D*IE Fledermaus (The Bat)* was first performed in Vienna at the Theater an der Wien on 5 April 1874. The first performance in Britain was at the Alhambra Theatre, London, in 1876; the American première took place in New York in 1879.

Famed throughout Europe as the "waltz king", Johann Strauss also had theatrical ambitions. Though his attempts at serious opera were total failures when performed, the sparkling comedy of *Die Fledermaus* and, to a lesser extent, of *Die Zigeunerbaron (The Gypsy Baron)* have ensured his operatic immortality. We are in a long-lost world – the world of *Kaiserlich und Königlich* Vienna, where all is laughter and gaiety, the waltz is king and Schlieffen has no plans.

ACT ONE Inside Eisenstein's house. Off-stage, the voice of Alfred, an old flame of Rosalinda, can be heard serenading her. Adele enters, reading a letter from her sister, Ida. The imperial ballet, of which Ida is a member, has been invited to a party to be given that evening by Prince Orlovsky, a wealthy Russian visitor to Vienna, and Adele can go with them. Rosalinda, who now enters, refuses to let her have the evening off to visit her sick aunt: that night Eisenstein is due to start a five-day prison sentence for flirting, and he must have a good supper before he leaves. Adele flounces out, and Alfred, who has been waiting his opportunity, enters. He, too, has heard of Eisenstein's approaching imprisonment and says he will take advantage of her husband's absence to call again later. Rosalinda consents, provided he will stop singing – she can resist anything, except the sound of Alfred's top A.

Quarrelling is heard outside and Eisenstein and his lawyer, Dr Blind, enter. Eisenstein is beside himself with rage. Not only was Blind responsible

CAST

Alfred
an opera singer
Tenor

Adele
the Eisensteins' maid
Soprano

Rosalinda
Eisenstein's wife
Soprano

Gabriel von Eisenstein
Tenor

Dr Blind
his lawyer
Tenor

Dr Falke
Eisenstein's friend
Baritone

Colonel Frank
the prison governor
Baritone

Prince Orlovsky
a wealthy Russian
Mezzo-soprano

Frosch
the prison gaoler
Speaking role

RIGHT **Eisenstein's attempts to flirt with the disguised Rosalinda backfire on him, when she sweeps off with his chiming watch, which he had been using to try to time her pulse.**

for his prison sentence in the first place, he says, but his brilliant advocacy has succeeded in having it raised from five days to eight. In a trio, Rosalinda grieves, Eisenstein rages and Blind rehearses the legal arguments he will use when he gets the chance to appeal.

Blind leaves, Rosalinda goes off to look for some old clothes for Eisenstein to wear in prison, and Dr Falke, a friend of Eisenstein's, enters. He is determined to exact vengeance for a practical joke that Eisenstein recently played on him and now embarks on the first stage of his plan. He invites Eisenstein to go with him, in disguise, to the Prince's party that evening and start his prison sentence the next morning instead. Rosalinda will never know. Nor does Falke tell Eisenstein that Rosalinda herself has received a similar invitation, which stipulates that she should attend the party disguised and masked.

Eisenstein is quick to accept his friend's sug-

gestion. Much to Rosalinda's amazement, he tells her he must leave at once, in full evening dress. Adele is given the evening off after all and Rosalinda is left alone to enjoy her assignation with Alfred. No sooner has Eisenstein departed than the amorous tenor is in the house, plying Rosalinda with wine, eating the supper that was prepared for Eisenstein and even donning the latter's slippers and dressing gown. The cosy scene is interrupted, however, by Colonel Frank, who has come to take Eisenstein off to prison. He, naturally enough, mistakes Alfred for his prisoner, despite the latter's denials. Rosalinda persuades Alfred, for the sake of her reputation, to go along with the bemused Frank, and the act ends with a brisk trio.

ACT TWO The party at Orlovsky's palace is in full swing, and the young prince urges everyone to enjoy themselves. Enter Eisenstein, disguised as the Marquis Renard. He feels sure that one of his

Die Fledermaus

LEFT Disguised as a Hungarian countess, Rosalinda sings a brilliant *czardas* to prove to the doubters among Prince Orlovsky's guests that she really is Hungarian.

RIGHT Eisenstein decides it is best to forgive and forget, and the entire company joins in a final chorus to celebrate the delights of champagne.

fellow-guests is Adele, but she and the company laugh at him for making such an obvious mistake. However, he completely fails to recognize Rosalinda when she arrives disguised as a Hungarian Countess. He immediately starts to flirt with her, pretending to time her pulse with his chiming watch, but somehow his plan goes wrong, and Rosalinda sweeps off triumphantly with watch and virtue intact.

Adele now suggests that the supposed Countess is not Hungarian at all and, to prove it, Rosalinda sings a brilliant *czardas*. This is the cue for the finale. Eisenstein and Colonel Frank, who has arrived disguised as the Chevalier Chagrin, toast one another with glasses of champagne, the toast leading on to a general oath of brotherhood and sisterhood for the entire company. The artists from the imperial ballet dance a waltz, after which the assembled company take over the dance floor. Suddenly, the revels are interrupted by the sound of a clock chiming six, and Eisenstein and Frank totter from the ballroom.

ACT THREE At the city prison in Frank's absence Frosch has been trying hard to match his master's alcoholic capacity, and is distinctly drunk. He is interrupted from time to time by snatches of song from the cell holding Alfred, and he eventually goes off to silence this nuisance. Frank, also much the worse for wear, returns and tries to settle down to sleep off his hangover. He is soon interrupted by Frosch, who is ready to make his morning report. The supposed Eisenstein has demanded

to see his lawyer, who is due to arrive imminently.

The door bell rings and two ladies are announced – Adele and her sister. Frank had taken a great fancy to them at the ball, and Adele begs Frank to help her in a stage career, saying that she will play any role he chooses. Another ring heralds the arrival of Eisenstein, who is still playing the role of the Marquis Renard. At first he thinks his friend, the Chevalier Chagrin, has been arrested, but, when he learns who the Chevalier really is, he thinks this a particularly good jest. Frank, for his part, laughs off the idea that the Marquis is really Eisenstein; he himself arrested the "real" Eisenstein at his home before going to the ball.

Another lady is announced and Frank goes out to greet her. In his absence, Eisenstein waylays Blind, who has also arrived, and borrows his glasses, wig and gown in the hope of finding out who it is that Frank has arrested.

The latest visitor is, of course, Rosalinda, who has come to see if she can get Alfred out of prison. Eisenstein, acting the part of Blind, starts to question the two of them, but eventually, unable to control his indignation any longer, he tears off his disguise. The rest of the company appear. Falke explains that he has succeeded in revenging himself on Eisenstein, and Rosalinda and Alfred are quick to add that their supper was all part of Falke's plot. Faced with the evidence of his own watch in Rosalinda's hand, Eisenstein decides it is best to forgive and forget, and all join in praising the healing power of champagne.

Strauss (1864–1949)

DER ROSENKAVALIER

Opera in three acts, libretto by Hugo von Hofmannsthal

Richard Strauss first won fame through his symphonic poems, such as Don Juan. He then turned to opera writing 15 in total, including Der Rosenkavalier, Salome (based on Oscar Wilde's play), in 1905, Elektra in 1907 and Ariadne auf Naxos in 1912. For many years, his later operas were generally held to be inferior to these, though many would argue that works such as Die Frau Ohne Schatten (The Woman Without a Shadow), Arabella and Capriccio are the equals of his early masterpieces. The last was premiered in 1942, at the height of World War II.

D ER *Rosenkavalier (The Knight of the Rose)* was first performed in Dresden on 26 January 1911. The first British and first American performances both took place in 1913, at the Royal Opera House, Covent Garden, London, and the Metropolitan Opera, New York, respectively.

In *Der Rosenkavalier* words and music combine to make the perfect operatic comedy of manners. After the excesses of *Elektra*, at the dress rehearsal of which he had called to the orchestra "Louder, I can still hear Frau Heink", Strauss went to considerable pains to ensure the audibility of the words, even though the opera is scored for an orchestra of over 100 players. Strauss, however, was not above rearranging the piece when the situation called for it; on his American visit in the early 1920s, he conducted reduced orchestras in selections from the score in department stores, much to the fury of musical purists, and the opera was the first to be filmed, back in the days of the silent cinema, with the vocal parts given to orchestral instruments!

ACT ONE A passionate prelude, depicting musically the love-making of Octavian and the Marschallin, leads straight into the first act. We are in the Marschallin's bedroom, where she is deep in conversation with her young lover. She says that he must take his leave of her but that she is as reluctant to release him as he is to go, for she believes the time is approaching when he will find a true love younger than herself. A noise is heard in the anteroom and both lovers take fright, thinking it is her husband, returning unexpectedly from a hunting trip. Octavian darts behind a screen, where he disguises himself as the Marschallin's maid, Mariandel.

CAST

Octavian
the Feldmarschallin's lover
Soprano

The Feldmarschallin
Princess von Werdenberg
Soprano

Baron Ochs von Lerchenau
her cousin
Bass

Major-Domo
Tenor

An Italian singer
Tenor

Valzacchi
an intriguer
Tenor

Annina
his partner
Mezzo-soprano

Herr von Faninal
a wealthy parvenu
Baritone

Sophie
his daughter
Soprano

Marianne
her nurse
Contralto

Faninal's Major-Domo
Tenor

A notary
Bass

An innkeeper
Tenor

Commissioner of Police
Bass

Chorus
Other supplicants in attendance at the Marschallin's levée, servants, intriguers, children, the Marschallin's page.

RIGHT The Italian tenor, accompanied by an on-stage flautist, sings a new aria to the Marschallin. All listen attentively, with the exception of Ochs, who eventually brings the performance to a close in typically heavy-handed fashion.

However, it is not as serious as the Marschallin had feared. She suddenly recollects that a country cousin, Baron Ochs, had written to say he would visit her that morning. This must be him, although he has arrived at an extremely anti-social hour. Ochs forces his way through the protesting servants into the bedroom, but immediately his attention is distracted by the pretty young maid, with whom he starts to flirt. Reluctantly, he is dragged back to the point of his visit. He had asked the Marschallin, as is the custom, to nominate a suitable knight of the rose to present a silver rose, the symbol of an engagement, to his chosen bride, Sophie von Faninal, the daughter of a wealthy and recently ennobled parvenu. He also wants the Marschallin to recommend a suitable lawyer, but she tells him to wait for her morning reception, which is about to start and which her own attorney will attend. In the meantime, Ochs resumes his shameless flirting with the supposed Mariandel, celebrating his pursuit of love.

The reception begins, and the stage fills with servants and supplicants for the Marschallin's favour. These include, as well as the Marschallin's lawyer, her chef, an Italian tenor, three noble orphans (plus their aunt), who have come to beg for charity, and two Italian scandalmongers, Valzacchi and Annina. They are soon joined by Ochs's down-at-heel servants, including his illegitimate son, Leopold, who bring him the silver rose.

While a hairdresser attends to the Marschallin's hair, the tenor sings an aria, with flute *obbligato*, to demonstrate his skills. Ochs is arguing with the lawyer – he cannot believe, he says, that he has to pay the Faninals a dowry rather than the other way around – and eventually interrupts the tenor at the climax of the second verse of his song. The levée comes to an end, and the Marschallin is left alone. She muses on the fate of this young girl, married so young to a lout such as Ochs and draws a parallel with her own arranged marriage. Not even the return of Octavian, dressed for riding, can change her sad mood and she repeats that, whatever he thinks now, he will leave her for a younger woman.

Octavian, wounded by this apparent mistrust, takes a formal farewell, but no sooner has he left the room than the Marschallin realizes she has not even kissed him. She orders her footmen to hurry in pursuit, but it is too late. Summoning her little black page, Mahomet, the Marschallin tells him to take the silver rose to Octavian. As she stares pensively into her mirror, the curtain falls.

ACT TWO A salon in Faninal's luxurious home. All is bustle as the family await the arrival of the

RIGHT Left alone, the Marschallin gives vent to her feelings about the lecherous behavious of her vulgar cousin. She goes on to reflect that her beauty, though great, is starting to fade, and that Octavian, too, will inevitably leave her.

BELOW Octavian, in full formal dress, enters to present Sophie with the silver rose. The Marschallin's previous forebodings are now fulfilled as the two fall rapturously in love.

knight of the rose. Sophie and her nurse, Marianne, are in a particular state of agitation. Shouts of "Rofrano" are heard from the street and, as the music reaches a climax, Octavian enters, carrying the silver rose in his hand. He formally presents it to Sophie, after which they talk together while they wait for the Baron to arrive. Both are taken with each other, but their talk is interrupted by Ochs, whose lack of manners and off-handedness Sophie finds extremely upsetting. As he continues to patronize her, making it clear that he is marrying her as a favour, Octavian's temper begins to rise, but, fortunately, the Baron is called into an adjoining room to finalize the marriage contract.

Left alone, Sophie expresses her loathing of her would-be bridegroom and, within moments, she and Octavian are in each other's arms. Valzacchi and Annina, anxious to prove their value to Ochs, surprise the young lovers and their shouts bring Ochs back on the scene. Octavian tells him that Sophie will never be his and eventually goads the reluctant Baron into drawing his sword and fighting him on the spot. A pin-prick wound is the result, but Ochs's reactions are enough to make everyone think he is dying. The furious Faninal tells Sophie that if she refuses to marry Ochs she will be sent to a convent, and the room clears. Ochs is left alone, drinking a recuperative glass of wine.

leave Octavian, dressed once again as "Mariandel", to meet the would-be seducer.

Ochs enters and supper is served. He plies "Mariandel" with wine, but Octavian keeps him at bay, pretending, at one stage, to be drunk and maudlin. As the exasperated Baron makes his move, Octavian stamps his foot loudly on the floor. Trapdoors and windows fly open in response and strange, ghostly figures appear. The superstitious Ochs is terrified, and his confusion is only increased when Annina, disguised as Och's deserted wife, bursts in, accompanied by his supposed children. Frantically, he calls for the police, but, when the Commissioner and his men enter, he can think only of pretending that "Mariandel" is his fiancée, Sophie von Faninal. This adds to his troubles, for, at that moment, Faninal, summoned by the intriguers, arrives. All Ochs can do is to pretend he does not know him, much to Faninal's irritation.

As the confusion rises to a height, the Marschallin, whom Leopold has run to for help, sweeps in, resplendent in full court dress. She quickly takes in the situation. The Commissioner, whom she recognizes as her husband's one-time orderly, is quickly persuaded that the whole affair was a practical joke, although Sophie, who has already told Ochs that neither her father nor she ever wants to see him again, is concerned that she, too, may have been a victim of the "joke".

Sophie, however, is soon reassured. Having dismissed Ochs, who runs off pursued by Annina, children, servants and creditors, the Marschallin turns to Sophie and Octavian and pushes the latter into Sophie's arms. She launches a great trio of renunciation and love, at its climax leaving the room to console Faninal. The lovers are left alone together. They sing a duet, interrupted by Faninal and the Marschallin's return. Faninal comments to the Marschallin how happy the two youngsters look, to which she simply replies "Ja, Ja". The lovers, after a moment, follow them to the Marschallin's carriage.

This is not quite the end of the opera, however. The sound of jingling bells is heard. Sophie has dropped her handkerchief and Mahomet has been sent back to find it. He snatches it from the floor, waves it in triumph and runs off after the others. The curtain quickly falls.

Octavian is still determined to win Sophie and hastily concocts a plan with the two intriguers, who are so disgusted with Ochs's refusal to pay them that they fall in with the Count's wishes. Annina therefore brings the Baron a note from "Mariandel", agreeing to an assignation that evening. The delighted Ochs waltzes around the salon in anticipation as the act comes to a close.

ACT THREE A brilliant orchestral fugue introduces the opera's last act, which is set in a private room in a disreputable inn on the outskirts of Vienna. Octavian has hired the chamber for the assignation with Ochs – but it is no ordinary room. As the landlord, Valzacchi and Annina demonstrate, it is fitted with secret trapdoors, blind windows and all sorts of tricks. As Ochs is heard approaching, they

GUISEPPE *Verdi* (1813–1901)

RIGOLETTO

Opera in three acts, libretto by Franceso Maria Piave after Victor Hugo's play Le Roi s'amuse

Guiseppe Verdi was forced to take composition lessons privately after being rejected as a student by the Milan Conservatory on the grounds that he was insufficiently talented. His first great success was Nabucco in 1842; subsequent operas firmly established him as the master of 19th-century grand opera, though, today, many would award the palm to his Don Carlos, originally written in French for the Parisians and later adapted for the Italian stage. After Aida, it took the two Shakespearean librettos prepared by Boito – Otello and Falstaff – to tempt him back to the theatre.

RIGOLETTO was first performed at the Teatro la Fenice, Venice, on 11 March 1851. The first performance in Britain was at the Royal Opera House, Covent Garden, London, in 1853; the American première was at the Academy of Music, New York, in 1855.

Verdi composed *Rigoletto* in an amazing 40 days, but, in common with many of his early operas, the subject brought him into conflict with the censors. The Austrians, then occupying Venice, objected to the depiction of a dissolute king (Francis I of France) on stage, as in Victor Hugo's play on which the opera is based. For this reason, the entire action was moved to the ducal court of Mantua, a dissolute duke being acceptable!

ACT ONE
SCENE 1
A brilliant ball is being held in the ducal palace. The Duke and Borsa enter, deep in conversation about a pretty girl the Duke has seen attending church. Although he does not know her name and despite the fact that a mysterious man visits her nightly the Duke is determined to pursue her. He sings of his cavalier attitude to women in general in the dashing aria "Questa o quella" ("This one or that one") and proceeds to dance the minuet with Countess Ceprano, another of his conquests, despite the fury of her husband, who looks on impotently.

Rigoletto, the Duke's hunchback jester, enters. He mocks Ceprano as a cuckold and then goes in search of other victims. Marullo joins the affronted Count with startling news. Despite his deformity, Rigoletto has a pretty young mistress. Ceprano and the other nobles, all of whom have suffered from the jester's barbed tongue, agree to meet the next night and revenge themselves by carrying her off.

A disturbance outside heralds the arrival of Count Monterone. Bitterly, he denounces the Duke

C A S T

The Duke of Mantua
Tenor

Borsa
a courtier
Tenor

Countess Ceprano
Soprano

Rigoletto
the court jester
Baritone

Count Ceprano
Baritone

Marullo
a courtier
Baritone

Count Monterone
Bass

Sparafucile
an assassin
Bass

Gilda
Rigoletto's daughter
Soprano

Giovanna
her nurse
Contralto

Maddalena
Sparafucile's sister
Mezzo-soprano

Chorus
Members of the Duke's court

Rigoletto

RIGHT The ball is interrupted by the arrival of the distraught Count Monterone, whose daughter the duke has dishonoured. When Rigoletto baits him, Monterone rounds on the duke and jester, cursing them both. Rigoletto is horrified when Monterone proclaims that he, too, will suffer the same fate.

BELOW As the revels at the ducal palace reach their height, the dissolute Duke of Mantua sings to his courtiers of the delights of love.

as the seducer of his only daughter. Rigoletto mocks him, but is struck dumb with terror as Monterone curses first the Duke and then the jester himself. "May everything that has befallen me happen to you," Monterone proclaims, as he is escorted to prison.

ACT ONE
SCENE 2 A street outside Rigoletto's house. The jester, still haunted by the thought of Monterone's curse, is joined by Sparafucile, who offers Rigoletto his services. The jester dismisses him, but takes note of where the assassin can be found.

Rigoletto sings of his fate – to be a jester who is never allowed to weep – of the love he has for his daughter and, again, of the curse that hangs over him. He enters his house to be greeted by Gilda. Protectively, Rigoletto questions her about her doings. She replies that she has not left the house, save to attend church. Rigoletto begs her not to mind his apparent possessiveness, explaining that since the death of his wife, Gilda is the only person for whom he cares. Gilda, for her part, tries to dispel his fears.

Their duet is interrupted by the sound of footsteps, and Rigoletto rushes off to see who is there. As he leaves, the Duke, in student dress, darts in through the door, tosses a purse to Giovanna,

Gilda's nurse, and hides. Rigoletto finishes his fare-wells to Gilda and leaves. Gilda sings of what she had not dared tell her father – of the handsome youth who had followed her home from church. Suddenly, that youth is at her side. He tells her he is a poor, but honest, student, and the two sing of their mutual love, only to be interrupted by the sound of footsteps. Hastily, they bid each other farewell.

Alone, Gilda muses on her new-found lover – "Caro nome" ("Dear name") – as she goes into her bedroom. As the aria reaches its conclusion, the whispering voices of the Duke's retainers are heard, come to carry out their plan. At that moment, Rigoletto himself reappears and they tell him that they are there to carry off Countess Ceprano (the Ceprano palace is just down the street). The jester agrees to help, but, instead of being masked, he is blindfolded and left holding a ladder, as the conspirators make their way into his home.

Rigoletto becomes impatient. He tears off the blindfold, realizes he has been duped and hurries to see if Gilda is safe. He returns with her scarf in his hands, which the conspirators have let fall in their flight. Monterone's curse has struck.

ACT TWO A room in the Duke's palace. The Duke is disconsolate, for, on his return to Rigoletto's home, he found it empty, with no trace of Gilda to be found. Marullo and the courtiers enter and explain their doings of the previous night to their master. The Duke, realizing that they, unknowingly, have brought Gilda to him, rushes to "console" her.

Rigoletto enters, feigning nonchalance. He cross-questions the courtiers, but their bland denials confirm his suspicions that they were all in the plot. Finally, he can contain himself no longer and, when they tell him to ask the Duke if he wants to know the whereabouts of his mistress, he demands to know what has happened to his daughter. Bitterly, he denounces them before pleading with them to take pity on a loving father. Shamefacedly, they turn away.

Gilda hurries into the room, and Rigoletto orders the courtiers to leave them. Once father and daughter are alone, she tells him the whole story, while he vainly tries to comfort her. Monterone is now led in, on his way to execution. His passage inspires Rigoletto to swear vengeance on the Duke, while Gilda pleads for mercy for the man whom, despite everything, she still loves.

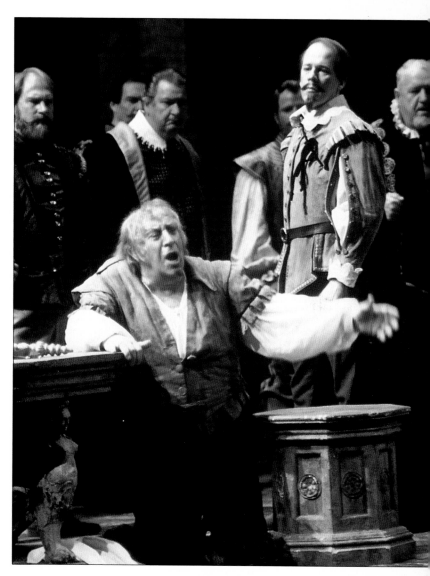

ABOVE Rigoletto, having denounced the duke's courtiers – "Cortigiani, vil razza dannata" ("You courtiers, vile, damned rabble") – pleads with them to help him find Gilda, his daughter and "only treasure".

ACT THREE A decrepit inn on the road outside Bologna, the home of Sparafucile and his sister, the flirtatious Maddalena. Rigoletto and Gilda enter. He has brought her there to witness the faithlessness of the Duke, who promptly appears, calls for wine and a room for the night and, catching sight of Maddalena, launches into one of Verdi's best known arias – "La donna è mobile" ("Fickle

Rigoletto

LEFT Inspired by Monterone's example, Rigoletto swears vengeance on the duke for having seduced his daughter, while Gilda pleads for forgiveness for the man whom, despite everything, she still loves.

BELOW Again in disguise, the duke flirts with Maddalena, Sparafucile's sister, while a broken-hearted Gilda and a grimly satisfied Rigoletto look on from their hiding place outside the inn. Rigoletto has arranged for Sparafucile to murder the duke.

is womankind"). He starts to flirt with Maddalena, who is by no means immune to his attractions although she pretends to repulse him, and while they flirt together, Gilda laments her betrayal and Rigoletto again swears vengeance.

Sparafucile emerges from the inn. Rigoletto pays him half his fee for killing the Duke; he will pay the rest when the body is delivered to him. He orders Gilda to return home, where she is to disguise herself as a boy and then make her way to Verona, where he will join her. Both leave.

A storm arises. The Duke retires to his room and Maddalena pleads with her brother to spare his life. As the storm reaches its height, their conversation is overheard by Gilda, who has returned to the inn in disguise. Maddalena urges Sparafucile to kill Rigoletto instead, but he replies that even assassins have their code of honour. Eventually he agrees that, if another male visitor arrives at the inn before midnight, he will slay him. Gilda sees the chance of saving the man she loves. As the clock strikes the half hour, she knocks at the door, saying she is a poor beggar seeking shelter. The door opens, she is admitted, and Sparafucile promptly strikes.

The storm has abated and Rigoletto returns. Sparafucile drags out a sack containing Gilda's body, takes his money and wishes the jester goodnight. Rigoletto gloats over the sack, but, as he prepares to hurl it into the nearby river, the Duke's voice breaks into song off-stage. Rigoletto tears open the sack to reveal his daughter. Pleading for forgiveness, she dies in his arms. Brokenhearted, Rigoletto exclaims that Monterone's curse has been fulfilled.

IL TROVATORE

Opera in four acts, libretto by Salvatore Cammarano from the Spanish drama by Antonio Garcia Gutiérrez

CAST

Ferrando
captain of Count di Luna's guards
Bass

Leonora
lady-in-waiting to the Princess of Aragon
Soprano

Inez
her confidante
Soprano

Count di Luna
Baritone

Manrico
a troubadour
Tenor

Azucena
a gypsy, Manrico's supposed mother
Mezzo-soprano

Ruiz
Tenor

Chorus
Soldiers, gypsies, nuns, ladies of the court

LEFT **Having mistaken the Count di Luna for her lover, the mysterious troubadour, in the darkness of the royal gardens, Leonora pleads for understanding.**

LEFT **Manrico and Leonora are together. Having found her with di Luna, he is quick to accuse her of betrayal. The count denounces the troubadour as a rebel, and the two men rush off to fight a duel.**

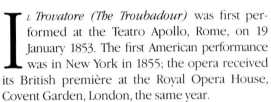

RIGHT **Manrico questions his supposed mother, the gypsy Azucena, about his real mother, but she tells him to ignore her ramblings, which, she says, were caused by a bad dream.**

I*L Trovatore (The Troubadour)* was first performed at the Teatro Apollo, Rome, on 19 January 1853. The first American performance was in New York in 1855; the opera received its British première at the Royal Opera House, Covent Garden, London, the same year.

According to Enrico Caruso, one simple factor was essential for a successful performance of *Il Trovatore* – the four greatest singers in the world in the leading parts. The story has frequently been criticized as over-complex, largely because so much of the action is supposed to have taken place before the curtain rises. However, Verdi's passionate music sweeps away any doubts with its sheer power and verve.

ACT ONE Ferrando and his men are on the
SCENE 1 watch, awaiting the return of their master, Count di Luna, who has gone to the palace to pay court to Leonora. To pass the time, the retainers encourage Ferrando to relate the grim events that took place 15 years

before. He obliges. The old Count di Luna had two sons. One morning, an aged gypsy was found by the cradle of the younger child, offering to cast his horoscope. Shortly after, the baby fell ill and, accused of witchcraft, the gypsy was burned at the stake. In revenge, her daughter stole the child and, or so it is thought, threw him into the flames (the charred bones of a dead child were found among the ashes of the pyre). To this day, Ferrando swears, he would recognize the murderess.

But this is not all. He goes on to tell his terrified companions that the old gypsy still haunts the castle, appearing in the form of an owl at midnight. As the clock strikes, all join in denouncing the witch.

ACT ONE In the gardens of the palace that
SCENE 2 same night Leonora tells Inez of her love for a mysterious knight, who first won her heart at a tournament and has been secretly serenading her in the gardens. As they retire, Count di Luna enters, but no sooner has he appeared than the song of the troubadour

is heard. Leonora returns, but, misled by the darkness, mistakes the Count for her lover. When the troubadour enters, Leonora realizes her error. He reveals himself as Manrico, a follower of Prince Urgel of Biscay, with whom the Aragonese are at war. Count and troubadour draw their swords and as they rush off to fight a duel, Leonora faints in terror.

ACT TWO
SCENE 1 A gypsy encampment in Biscay. Gypsies, working at their forges, sing the celebrated anvil chorus. Azucena, with Manrico lying beside her, reminisces about her mother's terrible death, adding to the story that Ferrando has already told that she herself had a child of the same age as the one she stole and, distraught by grief, cast her own son into the flames. When Manrico questions her, however, she tells him that her memory is playing her false and that he should pay no heed to her foolish babbling. She, in turn, has a question for him: why did he spare the Count when he had him at his mercy in their duel? Manrico replies that an inner voice told him to let his rival live.

A messenger from Manrico's friend, Ruiz, brings two letters with him. The first orders Manrico to take command of a fortress that is under threat from di Luna's troops; the second tells him that Leonora, believing him to be dead, is about to enter a nearby convent. Ignoring Azucena's desperate pleas to stay safe with her, Manrico hastens off to save his beloved.

ACT TWO
SCENE 2 The approach to the convent. The Count, who has also learned of Leonora's intentions, is waiting in the cloisters with Ferrando and a troop of soldiers to abduct her. He sings of his love.

A chorus of nuns heralds the approach of Leonora, accompanied by Inez and other ladies of the court. They are about to enter the convent when the Count intercepts them. At that moment,

however, Manrico, accompanied by Ruiz and his men, arrives on the scene. As Ruiz and his men hold the Count and his troops at bay, Leonora and Manrico escape.

ACT THREE
SCENE 1 The camp of the Count, who is laying siege to the fortress. Reinforcements are arriving, ready for the attack the next day. Ferrando, who has been raising the soldiers' spirits, announces that a gypsy woman has been apprehended nearby and Azucena is dragged forward. In response to the Count's questioning, she pleads that she is simply

ACT THREE
SCENE 2 Within the fortress Manrico and Leonora are about to be married, but Leonora has gloomy forebodings, which he is doing his best to dispel. As they prepare to make their way to the chapel, Ruiz bursts in to announce the news of Azucena's capture and imminent execution. Manrico immediately orders a desperate attack to rescue his mother.

ACT FOUR
SCENE 1 Manrico's attack has failed. The Count has taken the fortress and the gallant troubadour is himself under sentence of death. Ruiz and Leonora, both of whom managed to escape the fall of the fortress, enter. As the death knell sounds and Manrico and a chorus of monks intone the *Miserere*, Leonora proclaims that she will save her lover or die in the attempt.

The Count enters. He bargains with Leonora: if she will be his, he will order Manrico's release. Leonora agrees, but secretly swallows the poison she has concealed in her ring.

ACT FOUR
SCENE 2 Manrico's dungeon, in which Azucena is also confined. She is tormented by her memories and her approaching death; as she sinks into a stupor, Manrico tries vainly to comfort her. Leonora enters, bringing Manrico the news of his freedom, but, when she confesses that she cannot accompany him, he accuses her of treachery. Suddenly, she staggers as the poison begins to take effect. She admits what she has done and dies in the grieving Manrico's arms.

Leonora's death has been witnessed by the Count, who orders Manrico's immediate execution. He is led to the block, calling a last farewell to Azucena. As the headsman's axe falls, she reveals to di Luna that he has had his own brother slain.

a poor, wandering gypsy, but Ferrando finally recognizes her as the woman who abducted and murdered the Count's infant brother. As the Count orders her arrest, Azucena calls on her son, Manrico, to save her. The exultant Count sees the chance for a double revenge, and orders her to be burned at the stake.

LA TRAVIATA

Opera in three acts, text by Francesco Maria Piave after Alexander Dumas's play
La Dame aux Camélias

CAST

Doctor Grenvil
Bass

Baron Douphol
Baritone

Marchese d'Obigny
Bass

Flora Bervoix
Soprano

Gastone
Tenor

Violetta Valery
Soprano

Alfredo Germont
Tenor

Annina
Violetta's maid
Mezzo-soprano

Giorgio Germont
Alfredo's father
Baritone

Chorus
Servants, friends

LEFT As Alfredo's drinking song reaches its climax, Violetta and the chorus join him in praising the pursuit of pleasure and the joys of good wine.

L
A *Traviata (The Woman Led Astray)* was first performed at the Teatro la Fenice, Venice, on 6 March 1853. The first American and British performances took place in New York and London in 1856.

A failure on its first production in 1853, *La Traviata* is now one of the most popular operas in the repertory. In it, Verdi broke with convention by taking a "modern" subject, with characters in contemporary dress, even though many early stagings moved the action back in time to the days of Louis XIV.

ACT ONE At Violetta's Paris mansion a party is in full swing. Gastone, Alfredo's friend, tells Violetta, the beautiful hostess of the party, that Alfredo is in love with her and although she laughs this off, she is clearly touched by this devotion. The company calls on Alfredo to sing, and he launches a spirited *brindisi*, in which Violetta and her friends join. Music strikes up in an adjoining room, and the company moves off to dance, but, as Violetta makes to follow, she collapses with a coughing fit and sits down to recover. Alfredo, who has also remained behind, declares his love.

ABOVE Alone with Violetta, Alfredo declares his love for her, and she reveals how touched she is by his devotion.

RIGHT After Alfredo and his fellow guests have left her party, Violetta muses on what he has revealed. Dismissing her emotions as a momentary aberration, she bursts into a brilliant celebration of pleasure, only to be interrupted by Alfredo's off-stage voice, repeating his love song.

ABOVE Alfredo and Violetta have left Paris to set up home together in the country. Alfredo sings of the delights of their peaceful life together.

The two are interrupted by the returning guests – it is time to leave for another party and they hasten off, taking Alfredo with them.

Violetta is lost in contemplation. Alfredo's passion has touched her heart and she wonders if, by loving him, she can transform her way of life and find redemption. Suddenly, her mood changes. Such thoughts are total folly, and she launches into a brilliant celebration of a life of pleasure. But, as if to contradict her, Alfredo's voice is heard off-stage, repeating his serenade.

ACT TWO A room in a country house outside
SCENE 1 Paris, where Alfredo and Violetta have set up home together. Alfredo enters and sings of his joy, but his rapture is short-lived. Annina, Violetta's maid, tells him that, to keep up their establishment, her mistress has been selling her jewels secretly. He promptly leaves for Paris to raise the money to repay her.

Violetta enters, reading a note from her friend, Flora, asking her to a party that evening. Of course,

RIGHT Germont, Alfredo's father, arrives at the lovers' country retreat to plead with Violetta to give up his son before his association with a courtesan brings further disgrace not only on himself but on his innocent sister.

she has no intention of accepting. At that moment a visitor is announced. Violetta supposes that it is her business agent, whom she had been expecting, but the man who enters is a stranger. He asks her name and then reveals that he is Alfredo's father, come to plead with her to give up his son. Not only will their continued association doom Alfredo in society, but there is also his sister to consider. The scandal the affaire has caused has already led the family of her fiancé to break off her engagement. Violetta begs for understanding, and Germont is struck not only by her nobility, but by the fact that she is beggaring herself, rather than force Alfredo to support her. Finally, she yields to Germont's pleas, and the moved father leaves.

Summoning Annina, Violetta scribbles a hasty note to Flora and orders its immediate dispatch. She then sits down to write her farewell to Alfredo, telling him she is returning to her old life and to Baron Douphol, who has the means to support her, but she is interrupted by Alfredo's return. He tells her he expects his father to arrive, so she leaves the room so that father and son can be alone together. The passion of her farewell disturbs her lover.

A messenger arrives, with a note. Recognizing Violetta's handwriting, Alfredo tears it open, only to collapse into his father's arms as he reads it.

RIGHT Moved by Germont's pleas, Violetta eventually agrees to his request. She tells him that he can assure his daughter that her planned marriage can proceed, once she has renounced Alfredo.

G U I S E P P E   V E R D I
. . . .

La Traviata

RIGHT Denounced by Alfredo for having betrayed him by returning to her old life, Violetta sings of her hapless plight. Germont, knowing the extent of her sacrifice, reproves his son for his ungentlemanly behaviour.

Germont tries to console his son, but Alfredo is not to be comforted. He snatches up Flora's note and, swearing vengeance, rushes off to Paris. Germont follows.

ACT TWO **SCENE 2** Flora's mansion, where another party is in full swing. The guests, dressed as gypsies, are singing and dancing; they are joined by Gaston and his companions, dressed as matadors and picadors. Alfredo enters, shortly to be followed by Douphol, with Violetta on his arm. The two men gamble for higher and higher stakes, and Alfredo wins each hand – unlucky in love, lucky at cards. As the tension rises, a servant announces that supper is served in the next room.

The stage empties, but, a moment later, Violetta returns. She has asked Alfredo to join her, and, when he does so, she begs him to leave, fearing that the Baron's anger may lead to a duel. Alfredo accuses her of fearing for Douphol, rather than him, and, remembering her promise to Germont, she exclaims that it is Douphol she loves. Alfredo's fury boils over and, summoning the entire company, he denounces her for her faithlessness, flinging his winnings in her face. The company rounds on him, supported by Germont, who condemns his unworthy behaviour. An ensemble, in which Violetta sings of her love, closes the act.

ACT THREE Violetta's bedroom. She is in bed, attended by Annina. Sounds of carnival are heard from the street. Dr Grevil tells Violetta that she will soon recover but confides to Annina that her mistress has only a few hours to live.

Violetta, too, suspects the truth. Although Germont has written to tell her that Alfredo is aware of her sacrifice and is hurrying to her side, she exclaims bitterly that it is too late, and she sings a moving farewell to what her life might have been. At this moment, however, Annina excitedly announces Alfredo's arrival, and he bursts into the room, sweeping Violetta up into his arms. Nothing can part them: they shall leave Paris for some country retreat, where Violetta can regain her health. Violetta is suddenly racked with coughing, however, and falls back in a chair.

Grenvil has returned with Germont. They listen to Violetta's dying farewell. Suddenly, she exclaims she is feeling better and rises to her feet. It is the final crisis – she falls back dead, as Germont urges the distraught Alfredo to take courage.

AIDA

Opera in four acts, libretto by Antonio Ghislanzoni from the French prose of Camille du Locle, scenario by Mariette Bey

CAST

Radames
captain of the guard
Tenor

Amneris
the Pharaoh's
daughter
Mezzo-soprano

Aida
Amneris's Ethiopian
slave
Soprano

The Pharaoh
Bass

A messenger
Tenor

Ramphis
high priest of Egypt
Bass

Amonasro
Aida's father and
king of Ethiopia
Baritone

Chorus
Egyptian nobles,
warriors, citizens and
priests, slaves,
Ethiopian prisoners

LEFT Radames praises the beauty of Aida, Amneris's Ethiopian slave. Unknown to him and to everyone else at the Egyptian court, Aida is the daughter of the Ethiopian king, Amonasro.

IDA was first performed at the Teatro Italiano, Cairo, on 24 December 1871. It was first heard in Europe at La Scala, Milan, the following year, in New York in 1873 and in London in 1876.

Commissioned by the Khedive of Egypt for his new opera house in Cairo, the première of Aida was delayed for a year by the Franco-Prussian War. Although Verdi was ready with the score, the scenery and costumes were caught up in the siege of Paris and could not be shipped until the war had come to an end. This gave Verdi the opportunity to review what he had written, and the result is one of the grandest of grand operas that has fully stood the test of time.

ACT ONE SCENE 1 After a brief prelude (a latter revision, replacing a more conventional overture), the curtain rises on a hall in the royal palace at Memphis. Egypt is in danger. The Ethiopian king, Amonasro, has rallied his defeated army and launched it across the frontier to threaten Thebes. The priests are sacrificing to Isis to learn who should be appointed commander of the Egyptian forces.

The young warrior Radames hopes that he may be chosen, for, if he returns victorious, he can ask for the hand of Aida, the Ethiopian slave of Amneris, the Pharoah's daughter – "Celeste Aida" ("Heavenly Aida"). Aida and Amneris enter. In a duet, which later becomes a trio when Radames joins in, the Princess feigns friendship for her slave, but, in reality, because she is in love with Radames herself, she is jealous and suspicious of the one she believes to be her rival. King and priests enter with the news that Isis has spoken and has named Radames as the Egyptian commander. Amneris presents him with the royal standard, and, as the whole company joins in the cry of "Rittorna vincitor" ("return victorious"), he is led off to the sacred temple. Aida, alone, is filled with conflicting emotions. Although she has wished Radames well, by doing so she has betrayed her own people, and her father. For, although no one is aware of it, she is the daughter of Amonasro, the Ethiopian king. She prays to the gods to take pity on her.

ACT ONE SCENE 2 Ramphis, the high priest, and his followers are gathered at the temple, chanting solemnly in praise of the gods. Radames enters, and the priestesses perform a sacred dance. He is invested with consecrated armour, and the scene ends with a unison cry in praise of the god Phtah.

LEFT **The Pharaoh, Amneris, the people and the priests hail the return of the triumphant Radames, who parades his men and the booty they have captured before his royal master to the strains of a majestic march.**

BELOW **Amonasro is among the Ethiopian prisoners. He whispers to Aida not to betray him and tells the Egyptians that the Ethiopian king perished on the field of battle, asking them to show mercy to his fellow prisoners.**

ACT TWO SCENE 1 In the apartments of Amneris slave girls dance and sing. News arrives that Radames has triumphed, and Amneris resolves to use this to put Aida's feelings to the test. When her servant enters, Amneris tells her that Radames has been killed. Aida betrays herself through her grief, and Amneris explains that she lied and now knows the truth. Now, Aida shall know it, too – she has a rival and it is none other than Amneris herself. She orders her slave to accompany her to witness Radames's triumphant return.

ACT TWO SCENE 2 The entrance to the city. The Pharoah and Amneris enter to the cheers of the populace. A fanfare heralds the triumphal march of the victorious army, climaxed by the arrival of Radames himself, to be greeted by the Pharoah and crowned with a victory wreath by Amneris. As a reward, proclaims the Pharaoh, he will give Radames anything he desires.

Before making his request, Radames suggests that his prisoners are paraded before the royal couple. They are brought in, and Aida starts with terror as she recognizes her father in their ranks. With a muttered instruction not to betray him, as

LEFT Radames has unwittingly betrayed to Amonasro the route the Egyptian army will take, and he is sunk in shame at this dishonour. Amonasro and Aida vainly plead with him to fly with them.

he has not been recognized by his captors, Amonasro approaches the thrones. He tells the Pharoah how he saw the Ethiopian king perish on the battlefield and asks him to show mercy on those the Egyptians have conquered. The other captives, Aida and the Egyptian people join in the plea, but the priests demand that the captives be put to death. Finally Radames himself joins in the plea for clemency and reminds the Pharoah of his promise. The prisoners are ordered to be released, with only Amonasro being kept as a hostage. The Pharoah goes further: Amneris is to be Radames's bride. As the rest of the Egyptians rejoice, Radames and Aida are cast into despair.

ACT THREE   On the banks of the Nile. It is a beautiful moonlit night. A barge bearing Amneris and her attendants touches the shore and she enters the temple to seek the blessings of the gods on her forthcoming marriage. Aida stealthily enters and sings of her memories of her homeland, "O patria mia" ("My beloved country"). She is there to meet Radames, but, instead, it is her father who enters. He has discovered her secret and persuades

her that it is her duty to discover the line of the Egyptian army's advance so that he can escape and lead his forces from ambush. As Radames approaches, he retreats into the shadows.

Aida greets her lover coldly, but he reveals his secret plan. When he has won a further victory, he will ask the Pharoah to release him from his engagement and beg for Aida's hand. For her part, Aida counsels flight to her native land and such is the passion of her plea that Radames agrees. She asks him how they shall escape the Egyptian hosts and Radames names the planned route of advance, saying that it will be deserted until the morning. Amonasro exultantly echoes his words and reveals his true identity. Radames is horrified by his unintentional treachery, but king and daughter urge him to join them in flight.

Suddenly a cry of "traditore" ("traitor") bursts forth. Amneris and Ramphis have overheard them. As Aida and Amonasro escape into the night, Radames surrenders to the vengeful priests.

ACT FOUR   Amneris calls on the guards to SCENE 1   bring Radames before her. She pleads with him to repent and save his life, raging at his refusal to do so. He is led away to an underground chamber to stand trial. Amneris hears Ramphis accuse Radames of treason three times; each time the latter remains silent and the air resounds to a shout of "traditore" from the assembled priests. The sentence is that Radames is to be buried alive. Amneris begs vainly for mercy and hurls curses at those who have condemned Radames to die.

ACT FOUR   The setting is divided into two SCENE 2   floors, the upper one representing the interior of the temple and the lower Radames's sealed tomb. While Amneris and the priestesses kneel in prayer above, Radames prepares to meet his death. Suddenly, he sees a figure beside him – it is Aida, who has smuggled herself into the tomb. Finally united, the lovers raise their voices to heaven, while Amneris prays to the gods to give her peace of mind.

OTELLO

Opera in four acts, libretto by Arrigo Boito after William Shakespeare

CAST

Iago
Otello's ensign
Baritone

Roderigo
a Venetian
gentleman
Tenor

Otello
Tenor

Cassio
his lieutenant
Tenor

Montano
Venetian commander
in Cyprus
Bass

Desdemona
Otello's wife
Soprano

Emilia
Iago's wife and
Desdemona's
attendant
Mezzo-soprano

A herald
Bass

Lodovico
the Doge's emissary
Bass

Chorus
Soldiers, sailors,
ambassadors, people
of Cyprus

O*TELLO* was first performed at La Scala, Milan, on 5 February 1887. The American première took place at the Metropolitan Opera, New York, in 1888; the first British performance was at the Lyceum Theatre (visiting company from La Scala) the following year.

Otello is a remarkable opera, both for its music and for the compression of its construction. Between them, Verdi and Boito preserved the essence of Shakespeare and created a taut, compelling music-drama, in which words and music flow without a single extraneous moment. With great singing-actors in the leading roles and a great Verdi conductor in the pit, the opera makes an indelible impression, as in the Shakespeare tercentenary revival at the Royal Opera House, Covent

ABOVE The excitement mounts as Otello's ship is sighted, making its way through a wild storm to the safety of the harbour. Otello himself announces the successful rout of the Turks.

97

GUISEPPE VERDI

Otello

LEFT Iago proclaims his "Credo", ("I believe in a cruel god"). The idea for this outburst came from Boito, Verdi's librettist, rather than from Shakespeare.

RIGHT Otello is soon more than half-convinced by "honest" Iago that Desdemona is having an affair with Cassio, whose disgrace Iago has already contrived.

Garden, London, in which, at the last moment and without any stage rehearsal, the American tenor James McCracken made his British début in the title role, with Tito Gobbi as Iago and Sir Georg Solti as conductor.

ACT ONE The harbour of a seaport in Cyprus. Thunder and lightning roar and flash, and the orchestra conjures up the picture of a violent storm. The watchers on the shore, among whom are Iago and Roderigo, pray for Otello's safety. A cannon shot heralds the approach of his ship, and Otello bursts upon the scene. He proclaims the defeat of the Turks, and he is acclaimed by the crowd as he makes his way to the citadel. The Cypriots light a bonfire and gather around it to celebrate, laughing, dancing and drinking, while Iago and Roderigo talk together. We learn that Iago hates Otello because he has been passed over for promotion, which has gone instead to Cassio, while Roderigo is in love with Desdemona, Otello's wife.

The storm blows itself out, and Cassio, who had followed Otello to the citadel, returns. Iago starts a drinking song and plies Cassio with wine in a successful effort to get him drunk. The crowd laughs. Roderigo, whom Iago has set on to taunt Cassio, provokes the latter into a duel, and Montano

is accidentally wounded as he tries to intervene. Otello, who returns to quell the tumult, angrily dismisses Cassio from his lieutenancy.

The crowd disperses on Otello's command as Desdemona appears in search of her husband. The two sing of their love and embrace under the stars as the act comes to a close.

ACT TWO Within the citadel Iago, whose plan is now to make Otello suspect Desemona's fidelity, counsels Cassio to urge her to plead for his reinstatement. Alone, he sings of his belief in a cruel god, who has fashioned him in his own image. Seeing Otello approach, he comments on the favour Desdemona seems to be showing Cassio and, from this, starts to work his poison.

The scene between the two men is interrupted by a madrigal, in which a group of Cypriots present flowers to Desdemona. By its end, Otello has dismissed Iago's insinuations, only to have them immediately reawakened by Desdemona's ill-timed request for Otello to pardon Cassio. In the quartet that follows, Otello, Iago, Desdemona and Emilia express their conflicting emotions, and at the end Otello sends his wife to her room. As she leaves, she drops her handkerchief, which Iago is quick to pocket.

LEFT The bewildered Desdemona pleads with her husband to explain why he has turned against her, but Otello is now wholly determined on revenge.

BELOW Recalled by the Doge and Senate to Venice, Otello's fury is uncontrolled as he announces the name of his successor – Cassio.

Alone with Iago again, Otello bemoans his loss of peace of mind. Iago pretends to calm him, but his words have precisely the opposite effect. Roused to fury, Otello hurls him to the ground and threatens to kill him unless he can prove what he is hinting. Iago responds by telling Otello that he has heard Cassio talking of his love for Desdemona in his sleep and caps this by revealing that he has seen Desdemona's handkerchief, which Otello himself had given her, in Cassio's hands. Otello swears to avenge Desdemona's treachery, an oath in which Iago joins.

ACT THREE The great hall of the citadel. The imminent arrival of an emissary from the Doge is announced. Desdemona again pleads for Cassio's forgiveness, and Otello, in reply, demands that she should produce the handkerchief. When she fails to do so, he denounces her as a whore and strumpet. She vows her constancy, but eventually rushes terrified from the hall. Alone again, Otello soliloquizes about his problems until Iago hurries in, telling the Moor to conceal himself. Cassio is to hand and Iago will lead him on to discuss Desdemona. In the trio that follows, Otello half-hears enough to confirm his worst fears, although, in reality, Cassio is talking about another woman

Otello

altogether, especially when the ill-fated handkerchief is produced (Iago had previously hidden it in Cassio's room). As the ambassadors from Venice approach, Otello tells Iago that his mind is made up: he will kill Desdemona that night, while Iago promises to bring about Cassio's death.

The crowd hails the ambassadors. Their leader, Lodovico, hands Otello a dispatch from the Doge, which he reads and then orders Cassio to be summoned. Taunting Desdemona in a series of asides, he announces his recall by the Venetian senate and Cassio's appointment as his successor. Lodovico begs Otello to take pity on his weeping wife, but his reply is to hurl her to the ground. In a protracted ensemble, ambassadors and people call for mercy, but Otello is not to be moved. He dismisses the entire company before falling on the ground in a fit. Outside, the Cypriots hail the "lion of Venice", while the triumphant Iago spurns the prostrate, unconscious Otello with his foot.

ACT FOUR Desdemona's bedroom. Emilia is helping Desdemona get ready for bed. The latter sings the plaintive willow song, and the two women say their goodnights. Before retiring, Desdemona prays to the Virgin Mary.

The orchestral double-basses herald the arrival of Otello through a secret door. He wakes his wife with three kisses and then tries to force her to admit her guilt. As she pleads her innocence, he smothers her with her own pillow. Knocking is heard and Emilia runs into the room with the news that Cassio has killed Roderigo. Hearing a last dying whisper from her mistress, she denounces Otello as a murderer and screams for help. Cassio, Iago and Lodovico answer her summons and Emilia reveals the extent of Iago's villainy, a villainy confirmed by Montano, who enters bearing the confession of the dying Roderigo. Iago flees while Otello snatches up his sword from a table. Telling the company they have no need to hear him, he mourns his dead wife before stabbing himself. With a last call for a kiss, he dies as the curtain falls.

ABOVE Having publicly disgraced Desdemona in front of the Venetian ambassadors, Otello falls on the ground in a fit. It is the moment of Iago's triumph. He contemptuously scorns the prostrate Moor as, behind the scenes, the Cypriots praise the "lion of Venice".

LEFT Desdemona prepares to retire for the night. As she undresses she sings the plaintive willow song, following this with a prayer to the Virgin Mary to protect her.

FALSTAFF

Opera in three acts, libretto by Arrigo Boito after William Shakespeare

CAST

Dr Caius
Tenor

Bardolph and Pistol
Falstaff's followers
Tenor, bass

Sir John Falstaff
Baritone

Alice Ford
Soprano

Mistress Page
Mezzo-soprano

Mistress Quickly
Contralto

Nannetta (Anne)
Alice's daughter
Soprano

Ford
a wealthy burgher
Baritone

Fenton
in love with Nanetta
Tenor

Chorus
A page, servants, citizens of Windsor

ABOVE Bardolph and Pistol celebrate the greatness of Falstaff.

FALSTAFF was first performed at La Scala, Milan, on 9 February 1893. The first British performance was at the Royal Opera House, Covent Garden, London, in 1894; the American première at the Metropolitan Opera, New York, took place the following year.

Verdi claimed that *Falstaff*, his last opera, was written purely for pleasure, without thought or intention of public performance. Certainly, this product of his final year is unlike anything he had written previously. There are no great individual arias or set-piece ensembles – the whole opera is like a witty conversation, bubbling with life and zest from start to finish. Its completion also marked the consummation of Verdi's life-long love affair with Shakespeare, which, in operatic terms, had begun with *Macbeth* 46 years earlier.

ACT ONE In the Star and Garter Inn, Windsor, Falstaff and his cronies, Bardolph and Pistol, are fending off the indignant Dr Caius, who is complaining about their behaviour towards him. Failing to get satisfaction, he storms out, swearing never to get drunk again, save only in the company of honest men, to which Bardolph and Pistol reply with an antiphonal "amen".

SCENE 1

Falstaff, meanwhile, is examining his bill and looking at the contents of his purse, exclaiming that he is rapidly being reduced to beggary. Worse

RIGHT Over the teacups, the Merry Wives plot their vengeance on the presumptious fat knight. Mistress Quickly will be their go-between; by the time she has finished with Falstaff, he is sick of the sight of her.

BELOW Nannetta and Fenton are young and in love, but Ford has other plans for his daughter. Much to her dismay, he is determined to marry her off to the ageing, but wealthy, Dr Caius.

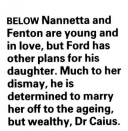

OPPOSITE Dressed in his wooing clothes, Falstaff preens himself before setting off to begin his first seduction.

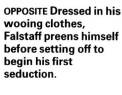

than this, starvation will mean loss of weight – and what will become of the imposing figure he has built up over the years? However, he has a plan to save the situation. He is currently enamoured of no fewer than two women, Mistress Ford and Mistress Page, the wives of two of Windsor's richest burghers. Bardolph and Pistol, he orders, shall take his love letters to them. Much to Falstaff's surprise, however, they flatly refuse; such a transaction is dishonourable. Falstaff despatches a page boy instead, and then rounds on the two recalcitrants. What do thieves and scoundrels such as they know about honour? At the end of his monologue, for which Boito took *Henry IV* as his source, he picks up a broom and chases them out.

ACT ONE The garden of Ford's house. The
SCENE 2 merry wives of Windsor, Alice Ford, Meg Page and Mistress Quickly, enter followed by Alice's daughter, Nannetta. Alice and Meg compare their notes from Falstaff and find them identical; they determine on revenge.

Ford enters on the other side of the garden, together with Caius, Fenton, Bardolph and Pistol. The servants have betrayed their master's intentions to Ford, who swears vengeance on Falstaff for having dared to contemplate seducing his wife. The men and women launch their own separate ensembles, which are intersposed with brief flirtations between Nannetta and Fenton. Both groups combined to end the act.

ACT TWO Back in the inn, a seemingly peni-
SCENE 1 tent Bardolph and Pistol present themselves to their master. They tell him that an old woman wants to see him, and Mistress Quickly bustles into the room. She curtsies deeply to the knight – musically mirrored by the orchestra – and tells him that she brings him messages from both Meg and Alice. Page is so jealous and possessive that he never leaves his wife on her own, but Alice Ford will be free to see him any afternoon between two and three. Falstaff assures her that he will certainly be there.

LEFT Falstaff assures Alice that, although he may have put on weight over the years, at heart he is as spritely as when he was the Duke of Norfolk's page.

Left alone, Falstaff is glorying in his impending triumph when another visitor is announced. It is Ford himself, going under the name of Master Brook (Signor Fontana). He has come to ask Falstaff for wooing lessons. He is in love with Mistress Ford, he says, and is willing to pay handsomely for the privilege. Falstaff airily assures him the deed is as good as done, for he has already arranged a rendezvous for that afternoon, and then he roundly abuses the character of Ford before going out to change. The furious Ford launches into a tirade on the subject of cuckoldry and jealousy. Falstaff returns and, after some disagreement about which of the two should go through the door first, they leave arm-in-arm.

ACT TWO SCENE 2 A room in Ford's house. The merry wives get ready to give Falstaff a reception he will never forget. Suddenly, they notice Nannetta is crying. She tells them that her father is determined she will marry the aged Caius, but she has set her heart on Fenton. Alice promises her to help her achieve her goal.

Mistress Quickly warns that Falstaff is approaching. The others hide while Alice starts to play the lute. Falstaff picks up the tune and uses it to sing her praises. He tells her that he was not always as she sees him now. When he was a young page to the Duke of Norfolk, he was slender and comely. He starts his great seduction, only to be interrupted by Mistress Quickly, who announces that Ford is unexpectedly returning. The knight is hastily concealed behind a convenient screen, just before Ford and his followers arrive and begin to search the house.

Taking advantage of Ford's temporary distraction, the women move Falstaff to a safer hiding place – a giant laundry basket, in which he is covered with piles of dirty washing. Ford returns in an even worse temper than before, when suddenly he hears the sound of kissing behind the screen. On the count of three, he and his followers knock

RIGHT Falstaff first conceals himself behind a screen, but finds a safer hiding place under a pile of dirty linen in a giant laundry basket. He gets more than he bargained for, however, when Alice orders her servants to empty the basket into the River Thames from the first-floor window.

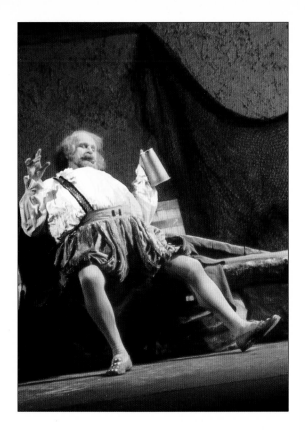

LEFT **Recovering from his ducking, Falstaff abuses the world for failing to appreciate a man of his quality. It takes a pint of good wine to make him take a mellower view of life. Verdi graphically depicts the wine's effects with a growing orchestral trill.**

RIGHT **Disguised as the Queen of the Fairies, Nannetta orders her "subjects" to beat and pinch Falstaff for having dared to interrupt their revels.**

the screen over, but instead of Falstaff and Alice, it is Fenton and Nannetta who are caught embracing.

While Ford rushes off again, Alice calls the servants and orders them to empty the laundry basket into the River Thames. Struggling under its weight, they do so. As Ford returns, Alice takes him to the window and points to the fat knight swimming for the shore. All enjoy the joke.

ACT THREE
SCENE 1
Outside the Garter Inn Falstaff is sitting, swathed in towels, railing against the world and how badly he has been treated. He calls for wine and starts to drink. This changes his mood, and he praises wine's powers to calm and console.

The merry wives and Ford (who is now part of their conspiracy) have not finished with Falstaff yet, however. Mistress Quickly re-enters, much to Falstaff's initial dismay, and persuades him that his ducking was a dreadful mistake. Alice will meet him again that evening on the stroke of midnight under Herne the Hunter's Oak in Windsor Forest. He is to disguise himself as the black hunter himself. Falstaff goes into the inn to prepare himself.

The women and Fenton plot the details of the evening's fun, while Ford tells Caius that he, too, has a plan – he will announce the latter's betrothal to Nannetta that very night. They are overheard, however, and the wives, off-stage, begin to devise a counter-stratagem as night and the curtain falls.

ACT THREE
SCENE 2
In Windsor Forest that night Fenton sings of his love for Nannetta before the rest of the conspirators arrive. Disguises are hastily donned – Nannetta is dressed as the queen of the fairies – and they conceal themselves as Falstaff arrives on the scene.

Midnight strikes and Alice enters, but no sooner has she appeared than she vanishes, leaving Falstaff alone to face Nannetta, who, as queen of the fairies, calls on her followers to punish the rash knight for having dared to intrude on their revels. All join in pinching and beating the cowering Falstaff, until the tormented victim suddenly recognizes Bardolph by his long nose. As the conspirators unmask, the extent of Falstaff's humiliation is revealed, but he rises to the occasion by announcing that, without him, their joke would have been pointless.

Ford announces Nannetta's betrothal to Caius and then does the same for another masked couple, whom Alice brings forward. They are unmasked and Caius finds himself betrothed to Bardolph while Ford discovers that he has unwittingly consented to the marriage of Nannetta and Fenton. Falstaff teases him – who is the dupe now? Alice proclaims all three – Falstaff, Ford and Caius – equally guilty, and Ford is induced to bless his daughter, and Falstaff leads the entire company in a final chorus, praising the power of a good jest.

Wagner (1813–83)

TRISTAN UND ISOLDE

Opera in three acts, libretto by the composer

Richard Wagner revolutionized opera through a series of vast, symphonically conceived music-dramas, and his use of leit motifs. In 1848, his role in the Dresden uprising forced him into exile, and scandal and poverty continued to dog his career until, in 1864, King Ludwig of Bavaria befriended him and became his patron. The opera house Wagner later built at Bayreuth to stage his Ring cycle is still home to an annual festival devoted to his works every year and is still controlled by his descendants.

Tristan *und Isolde (Tristan and Isolde)* was first performed at the Royal Court Opera, Munich, on 10 June 1865. The first performance in Britain was at the Theatre Royal, Drury Lane, London, in 1882; the opera was first staged in America at the Metropolitan Opera, New York, in 1886.

"The ripest fruit from a 'tree of good and evil', especially evil," was how one leading critic described *Tristan und Isolde* on its first London performance in 1882. In common with all Wagner's mature operas, *Tristan* was much misunderstood when it first appeared. The Viennese critic Eduard Hanslick even attacked the language of the libretto, over which the composer had taken considerable pains, as ridiculous, notably the play on the word *und* (and) in the great love duet in the second act.

In fact, at the first performance, physical love was present on stage, since the Tristan and the Isolde were married. The death of the former from influenza shortly after the première devastated Wagner, who, for a time, held that no other singer could possibly sing the part successfully.

ACT ONE The prelude leads straight into the first act, set on Tristan's ship, which is carrying Isolde back to Cornwall to marry King Marke, the young knight's uncle. Isolde and her attendant, Brangäne, are discovered listening to a young sailor who, from high in the rigging, is bidding farewell to his "Irish maid". Isolde asks Brangäne the vessel's course. When she learns that Cornwall is close at hand, she invokes the elements to destroy ship, passengers and crew, particularly Tristan, who, she says, has betrayed her. Listening with growing impatience to Brangäne's praise for the Cornish hero, she orders her to summon Tristan to her presence. He, however, refuses to leave the helm, and when Brangäne repeats her mistress's com-

CAST

A young sailor
Tenor

Isolde
an Irish princess
Soprano

Brangäne
her attendant
Mezzo-soprano

Tristan
a Cornish knight
Tenor

Kurwenal
his retainer
Baritone

King Marke
ruler of Cornwall
Bass

Melot
a courtier
Tenor

A shepherd
Tenor

Chorus
Sailors, knights,
esquires, soldiers

mand, Kurwenal, Tristan's retainer, answers her by breaking into a song in his master's honour.

Isolde, angered even more by this, now reveals the reason for her fury. She tells Brangäne how Tristan, who had killed her lover but had been wounded in the fight, came to Ireland to seek her help (she is a mistress of the healing arts). She had determined to kill him, but fell in love with him instead and nursed him back to health. Before he left the Irish court, he vowed eternal gratitude – and this is how he is now repaying her.

Brangäne urges Isolde not to despair and draws her attention to the love potion in her travelling casket. Isolde's eyes, however, light on a phial containing deadly poison. As sailors are heard greeting the sight of land, she quickly formulates a plan. Bidding Kurwenal summon Tristan to her presence, she orders Brangäne to mix the poison in a goblet of wine. The traitor shall perish, after which Isolde will take her own life.

Tristan finally enters. Claiming she wants him to drink a toast of reconciliation, Isolde hands him the goblet, which he half drains. Isolde finishes the draught. The two stare into each other's eyes, until suddenly the spell is broken and Isolde sinks into Tristan's arms. Brangäne has disobeyed her mistress's instructions and the two have drunk the love potion. As the ship docks and knights and courtiers flock on board to hail the valiant Tristan, Isolde faints in his arms.

ACT TWO It is night in the garden of King Marke's stronghold. In the distance, hunting horns are heard. Brangäne appears on the steps leading to Isolde's room. Beside her is a flaming torch, and extinguishing this is the signal to Tristan that all is safe and he may approach. Brangäne, however, is full of foreboding. As Isolde impatiently asks if the signal can now be given, she warns her mistress that she suspects Melot, a courtier, of treachery, but Isolde laughs off these fears. Even Brangäne's confession that she substituted the love potion for poison has no effect, and eventually Isolde herself puts out the torch.

Tristan appears and the two lovers rush into each other's arms. In a rapturous duet, they pour out their love for one another – "O sink hernieder, Nacht der Liebe" ("Oh sink upon us, night of love") – interrupted only by Brangäne's voice warning them that daybreak is near. The lovers ignore her

LEFT **Isolde has ordered Brangäne to poison the wine she is going to offer Tristan and then drink herself but unknown to her, Brangäne has substituted a love potion for the poison.**

BELOW **Tristan and Isolde meet secretly in the gardens of King Marke's castle, swearing their undying love in one of Wagner's greatest duets.**

Tristan und Isolde

LEFT **Kurwenal tries to comfort his dying master. He has sent a ship for Isolde, and she is sure to arrive shortly.**

RIGHT In the *Liebestod*, Isolde mourns the fallen Tristan before falling dead by his side as the music reaches its climax.

until a cry is heard, and Kurwenal rushes in, urging his master to save himself. But it is too late, for close behind come the King and his courtiers, led by the treacherous Melot. Marke reproves his young kinsman, who responds by asking Isolde if she is prepared to share his exile. As she consents, Melot draws his sword. Tristan hurls himself on him, but, as Melot thrusts, Tristan lets his guard drop. As he falls to the ground, Isolde throws herself on her wounded lover's body.

ACT THREE Outside Tristan's castle. Tristan is prostrate, apparently lifeless, with the faithful Kurwenal at his side. A shepherd, watching the sea, reports that there is, as yet, no sign of the ship Kurwenal has sent to Cornwall to watch Isolde.

Tristan slowly wakens. Kurwenal tries to comfort him by saying that Isolde will soon arrive, but

he is rapidly approaching delirium. As the shepherd signals the arrival of the ship and Kurwenal goes off to greet Isolde, Tristan tears off the bandages covering his wounds. No sooner have the two lovers greeted each other than the exhausted Tristan falls lifeless at Isolde's feet.

Another ship arrives, bearing Marke, Melot and their followers. Kurwenal and his men attack them, but are overpowered, the mortally wounded Kurwenal falling dying at his dead master's side. His one consolation is that Melot, too, has perished in the fight.

Brangäne tries to tell Isolde that she has confessed to the King that she gave the ill-starred lovers the love potion and he has come to forgive them, but it is too late. Isolde seems in a trance. She launches herself into a long farewell to her lover – and to life. As the *Liebestod* reaches its climax, she falls lifeless on Tristan's corpse.

DIE MEISTERSINGER VON NÜRNBERG

Opera in three acts, libretto by the composer

CAST

Walther von Stolzing
a young knight
Tenor

Eva
Pogner's daughter
Soprano

Magdalene
Eva's companion
Mezzo-soprano

David
Sachs's apprentice
Tenor

Veit Pogner
a goldsmith
Bass

Sixtus Beckmesser
town clerk
Baritone

Kunz Vogelgesang
a furrier
Tenor

Konrad Nachtigal
a tinsmith
Bass

Hans Sachs
a cobbler
Bass-baritone

Fritz Kothner
a baker
Bass

Hermann Ortel
a soap boiler
Bass

Balthasar Zorn
a pewterer
Tenor

Augustin Moser
a tailor
Tenor

Ulrich Eisslinger
a grocer
Tenor

Hans Foltz
a coppersmith
Bass

Hans Schwarz
a stocking-weaver
Bass

Nightwatchman
Baritone

Chorus
People of Nuremberg

D IE *Meistersinger von Nürnberg (The Mastersingers of Nuremberg)* was first performed at the Royal Court Theatre, Munich, on 21 June 1868. The British première took place at the Theatre Royal, Drury Lane, London, in 1882; the first American performance was in 1886 at the Metropolitan Opera, New York.

Die Meistersinger is Wagner's only comic opera, and unlike many of his other works, it breathes the air of real, human life. The historical Hans Sachs lived in Nuremberg from his birth in 1494 until his death in 1576; he is said to have written some 6,000 poems.

One character, however, is not based on medieval Nuremberg life. This is Sixtus Beckmesser, the bigoted town clerk, whom Wagner maliciously

ABOVE Eva, fresh from church, is eager to greet the handsome young knight, Walther von Stolzing, whom she met previously when he visited her father's shop.

Die Meistersinger von Nürnberg

RIGHT Sachs takes down the words of the new prize song that Walther von Stolzing dreamed the previous night.

BELOW Following the riot at the end of Act 2, the Nightwatchman re-enters to call the hour as the city returns to its slumbers.

modelled on the Viennese critic Eduard Hanslick, his bitter opponent. Indeed, in an early draft of the libretto, Beckmesser was actually called "Hans Lick", a fact not lost on the critic, who, having been invited to a private reading of the libretto, walked out after the first act.

ACT ONE A prelude, in which some of the main musical motifs of the opera are rehearsed, leads straight into Act 1. Inside the Church of St Catherine in medieval Nuremberg the congregation is singing the final chorale of the service. Walther von Stolzing, who is visiting the city to do business with Pogner, has seen and fallen in love with the goldsmith's daughter, Eva, and has followed her to church. As the service ends and the congregation emerges, Eva pretends she has left her prayer book in her pew and sends Magdalene, her companion, to look for it so that she can speak with the stranger. The two immediately declare their love for each other, but Magdalene, whose attention has been distracted by the arrival of her sweetheart, the apprentice David, tells Walther that Pogner is giving Eva's hand, together with his entire fortune, to the winner of the singing contest that is to be held the next day. This contest is open only to members of the Mastersingers Guild.

Walther asks what this guild is and what its

RIGHT The citizens of Nuremberg gather on the banks of the Pregnitz for the celebrations that will mark St John's feast day and also to see Eva betrothed to the man who carries off the Mastersingers' prize.

rules are. David explains, although he is interrupted by the noise of his fellow apprentices setting out for the singing school. Suddenly, they fall silent as the Mastersingers themselves approach, Pogner and Beckmesser leading the way. Walther begs leave to be admitted to their number, gaining the immediate enmity of Beckmesser, a prickly pedant who himself intends to compete for Eva's hand. Pogner outlines his plan to the assembled Master-singers. The only dissenting voice is that of Sachs, who urges that the people, too, should be given a voice, but his suggestion is overridden.

Walther is now ready for his test, and Beck-messer, the Mastersingers' assessor, enters the marker's booth and shouts to him to begin. He sings an impassioned song about the beauties of spring and love, but its ardent cadences find little favour with the Mastersingers, least of all with Beckmesser, who bursts indignantly from his booth with his slate covered with chalk marks. Despite Sachs's pleas for tolerance, they mock the knight as he continues to sing. The apprentices join in the hubbub until Walther is finally silenced, and the outraged Mastersingers stalk from the church.

Only Sachs is left behind for a moment. He pensively looks at the singer's chair, then, with a shrug of his shoulders, follows his brethren out onto the street.

ACT TWO The square outside Sachs's cob-bler's shop, the night before the Midsummer fes-tival. Pogner's house is next door. David and his fellow apprentices are shutting up shop for the night. David is teased about his love for Magdalene, who enters to learn that Walther was rejected. She hurries back to Pogner's house to break the news to Eva. David and the rowdy apprentices are on the brink of coming to blows when Sachs enters, sends the apprentices smartly on their way and takes David into the shop.

Pogner and Eva return from an evening stroll. He asks if she understands her role in the next morning's ceremony, but she manages to avoid giving a direct answer. Magdalene takes advantage of her mistress's return to break the news of Walther's misfortune, and Eva resolves to seek Sachs's advice. She finds him musing on the very subject. At first, she conceals from him her interest in Walther, inveigling her way into his favour by suggesting that he, a widower, should himself enter the contest for her hand. Unaware of the depth of Sachs's unselfish love for her, she eventu-ally reveals her affection for the young knight. Sachs pledges himself to work secretly for their

LEFT Beckmesser, tormented by nerves, is the first to sing, but he cannot even remember the words of the song Sachs let him have, while the music he has chosen to set them to is totally unsuitable.

OPPOSITE LEFT Walther, dressed for the festival, launches into the song that is going to win him the singing contest, Eva's hand and membership of the Mastersinger's guild.

union. He retires into his shop as Eva learns from Magdalene that she is soon to be serenaded by Beckmesser, and the two agree that Magdalene shall impersonate Eva at her window.

Walther arrives in search of Eva. Now that he has failed at the singing contest, he says, the only course left open to them is to elope. Sachs, who has overheard them, tries to prevent this, believing that there must be a better alternative. As the lovers hide in the shadows, the Nightwatchman crosses the scene, closely followed by Beckmesser, who is equipped with a lute and ready to begin his serenade. He is dismayed to find Sachs, who has emerged from his shop, hammering busily at his own new shoes, which, Sachs says, must be ready for Beckmesser to wear at the contest. Eventually, they agree on a compromise. Beckmesser will be allowed to sing, provided that Sachs may mark each fault with a hammer blow.

Magdalene appears at the window disguised as Eva, and the serenade starts. Sachs, as marker, is just as severe on Beckmesser as the latter had been on Walther; as Beckmesser desperately sings louder and louder, the hammer blows resound

faster and faster, until the whole street is roused. David, furious at finding Beckmesser serenading, as he thinks, Magdalene, sets about the luckless town clerk with a cudgel, and soon a riot is in full swing. Taking advantage of the confusion, Sachs pushes Walther into his shop, while Pogner reclaims Eva, whom he has taken for Magdalene. The noise subsides, and the Nightwatchman re-enters to call the hour as the act comes to an end.

ACT THREE Sachs is reading in his workshop, as David returns from delivering
SCENE 1 Beckmesser's new shoes and from making his peace with Magdalene. He wishes his master a happy birthday. Alone again, Sachs reflects on human unpredictability, which he resolves to turn to good account as far as Eva and Walther are concerned. The knight enters and tells Sachs of a song that came to him in his sleep, and Sachs urges him to sing it, taking down the words as he does so. The two retire to prepare themselves for the festival.

Beckmesser enters, still limping from his beating and determined to reprove Sachs for his part

BELOW Gathered around the singer's dais, the citizens of Nuremberg hail Walther's prize song. At first, he rejects the offer of membership of the Mastersingers, but yields when Sachs explains the significance of the guild as the upholder of German art and culture.

in the happenings of the previous evening. He finds the unfinished song and jumps to the conclusion that it is the work of Sachs himself, who will sing it in the competition. Sachs denies any such plan, and to prove it, he gives the song to Beckmesser, saying he can sing it himself. The overjoyed clerk hurries off, as Eva enters, complaining that her new shoes are pinching. Walther enters, dressed for the festival, and the sight of his love inspires him to finish his song. Eva thanks Sachs for his generosity of spirit and, with Magdalene and David, whom Sachs now releases from his apprentice indentures, they sing a quintet of joy and celebration.

ACT THREE

SCENE 2

An orchestral interlude leads directly to the opera's final scene, set on the banks of the River Pegnitz. The citizens greet the members of the city's guilds. A dance is interrupted by the ceremonial entrance of the Mastersingers themselves. The loudest cheers are for Sachs, and the assembled Mastersingers, guildsmen and citizens sing the hymn he himself had composed in honour of Martin Luther.

Sachs introduces the contest with a paean of praise for the giver and the prize, and Pogner replies. Now Beckmesser starts to sing. He has been unable to memorize the song and is tormented by nerves. His efforts are rewarded by jeers. Angrily, he tells the crowd that the song they have dismissed was not written by him, but by their beloved Sachs. Sachs replies that he can prove he is not the author and, also, that there is nothing wrong with the song when it is sung as its writer intended. He bids Walther, as the real author, to sing the song as it should be sung. It is greeted with acclamation.

Only one thing is needed to regularize the situation – Walther must be made a Mastersinger at once. At first, remembering his previous humiliation, Walther rejects the honour, but Sachs tells him he must acknowledge the Mastersingers' role as custodians of art and its renewal.

Walther relents, Eva crowns Sachs with a laurel wreath, and the entire company sings his praises and those of the culture of which the Mastersingers are the keepers.

DER RING DES NIBELUNGEN

A stage-festival play for three days and a preliminary evening, libretto by the composer.

The *Der Ring des Nibelungen (The Ring of the Nibelung)* was first performed complete at Bayreuth, Germany, on 13, 14, 16 and 17 August 1876. The first British performance was at Her Majesty's Theatre, London, in 1882; the American première took place at the Metropolitan Opera, New York, in 1889. *Das Rheingold (The Rhinegold)* was first heard at the Royal Court Opera, Munich, on 22 September 1869; the same theatre staged the première of *Die Walküre (The Valkyrie)* on 26 June 1870.

Der Ring des Nibelungen is not only the most epic of all epic opera cycles in terms of actual performance, but the story of its composition is also an epic in its own right. Wagner made his first sketches as early as the autumn of 1848, when he started work on a scenario entitled *Siegfried's Tod*, which later became the basis for *Götterdämmerung (The Twilight of the Gods)*. This was followed by a further sketch for *Siegfried* and Wagner then went on to add *Die Walküre* and *Das Rheingold*. The text of the music dramas was actually published in 1863, but it was not until 1869, through the intervention of Ludwig II of Bavaria, that *Das Rheingold* was physically performed.

By this time, Wagner had determined that a special theatre should be built specifically for the first performance of the complete cycle. This was eventually staged in 1876, 28 years after the *Ring's* inception.

RIGHT The Rhinemaidens salute the gold they guard as the Nibelung Alberich looks on in wonder. If the owner renounced love, they tell him, a ring could be forged that would ensure that its wearer would dominate the world.

DAS RHEINGOLD

Prologue in four scenes to the trilogy Der Ring des Nibelungen

SCENE 1 ——— A soft, unison chord of E flat on the double-basses signals the start of the prelude that takes us down to the depths of the river Rhine. There, the three Rhinemaidens are discovered swimming around a central ridge of rock, delighting in their freedom. Enter Alberich, coughing and sneezing. Lured by the Rhinemaidens' beauty, he struggles to climb their rock to catch them as they tease him, but he becomes increasingly angry and frustrated as they slip away.

Rays of light penetrate the water, revealing the gold the Rhinemaidens guard. The Rhinemaidens salute the gold and sing of the power it would possess were it to be stolen and forged into a ring. But, they say, no one would be prepared to make the sacrifice this would require, for the ring could be forged only by someone prepared to renounce love eternally. Alberich, after a moment of reflection, feverishly begins to climb towards the gold. Snatching it in his hands, he proclaims that he is

CAST

Woglinde, Wellgunde and Flosshilde the Rhinemaidens *Soprano, soprano, contralto*	**Fasolt and Fafner** the giants *Bass, bass*
	Froh *Tenor*
Alberich ruler of the Nibelungs *Bass-baritone*	**Donner** *Bass*
	Loge god of fire *Tenor*
Fricka Wotan's wife *Mezzo-soprano*	
	Mime Alberich's brother *Tenor*
Wotan ruler of the gods *Baritone*	**Erda** *Contralto*
Freia *Soprano*	

prepared to forgo love for ever, and he vanishes, pursued by the Rhinemaidens who swim after him vainly calling for help.

SCENE 2 An orchestral interlude leads straight into the next scene. Wotan and Fricka are discovered asleep, the towers of the newly built stronghold of Valhalla visible in the background. Fricka wakes and calls in surprise to Wotan, who emerges from his dreams to sing of the glory of his new home. Fricka, however, reminds him that there is a price to pay: in order to get the giants to build him the castle, Wotan promised to give them Freia, the goddess of youth, as a reward. Wotan replies that he had never intended to keep the bargain. With the aid of Loge, the god of fire, he means to trick the giants and save Freia from her fate.

No sooner has Wotan made this pledge than the terrified Freia runs in, pursued by Fasolt and Fafner. They insist that Wotan honour his bargain, but he tries to temporize until Loge arrives. In the meantime, Donner and Froh arrive to rescue their sister. When Loge enters, he tells the assembled company of gods and giants of the theft of the Rhinegold and the powers that have accrued to Alberich since his successful forging of the ring.

The two giants confer, Fafner urging his brother to agree that the ring and the treasure it has been used to amass should be substituted for Freia. Wotan, at first, refuses this demand, for he is determined to win the ring for himself. The giants carry Freia off, saying they will return that evening for the gods' final decision.

As soon as Freia has disappeared, the gods appear to age visibly. Without her and her golden apples they will lose their immortality, and they beg Wotan to descend with Loge into Alberich's underground kingdom to wrest the ring and gold from him and to ransom Freia. Eventually, he consents.

SCENE 3 A violent orchestral interlude graphically depicts the descent of the two gods into Nibelheim. The hammers of Alberich's subject dwarfs are heard hard at work until their noise eventually fades away. Alberich enters, dragging his brother Mime after him. Mime is carrying a helmet, which Alberich immediately snatches. This is the tarnhelm, which makes its wearer able to change himself into any creature, or even to

make himself invisible. To test its power, Alberich transforms himself into a column of steam and sets about Mime with his whip. He leaves, still invisible, to give his orders to his terrified subjects.

Mime is joined by Wotan and Loge, and the dwarf tells them how his brother has become all-powerful. Alberich returns, driving before him a band of Nibelungs, laden with gold and silver. Noticing the two gods, he abuses Loge for having allowed strangers to enter Nibelheim and then orders the Nibelungs to descend into the lower caverns to dig out more treasure. When they hesitate, he stretches the ring menacingly towards them and they flee in terror, together with Mime.

Wotan and Loge set out to flatter the suspicious dwarf, telling him that they have heard reports of his wealth and power and have come to see if they are true. Alberich boasts that, with the power of the ring, he and his hosts will soon emerge into the daylight and the whole world, including the gods, will come under his sway. Loge asks for a demonstration, and the dwarf dons the tarnhelm, transforming himself into a huge serpent. Loge asks if he can transform himself into something small, and the gullible Alberich promptly changes himself into a toad. Wotan quickly puts his foot on him. Loge pulls the tarnhelm off Alberich's head, the two gods bind their furious prisoner and carry him off up through Nibelheim and into the open air.

SCENE 4 Back on the surface, Loge and Wotan triumphantly emerge with their prisoner. They mock Alberich and tell him that, to win his freedom, he must command the Nibelungs to disgorge his golden hoard. Reluctantly, the dwarf consents and the treasure is brought to the surface. He is forced to surrender the tarnhelm as well, but mutters that he can re-create what he has lost as long as he retains the ring. This hope is soon crushed, however, when Wotan demands that he relinquish it, and, after a struggle, the god tears the ring from the dwarf's finger and puts it on himself. Contemptuously, Alberich is told he is free to go. To music of sinister power, he curses any future wearer of the ring before vanishing.

It starts to grow lighter and the giants are sighted, returning with Freia. It is agreed that she must be concealed by the stolen treasure, and Donner and Froh begin to pile up the hoard. Freia is still not totally concealed, even when the tarnhelm is added to the heaped treasure. A streak of

ABOVE The gods prepare to enter their new home, the fortress of Valhalla, across the rainbow bridge Donner has forged with the aid of a timely thunder bolt. As they advance, however, the voices of the Rhinemaidens bewailing their lost gold are heard.

her golden hair can still be seen.

Loge asks what more the gods can surrender – the gold is exhausted. By no means, Fafner replies. The golden ring he can see on Wotan's finger is surely part of the hoard. Loge tells him that this must be returned to the Rhinemaidens, but Wotan contradicts him, saying that he will keep the ring for himself. The giants reply that the original bargain stands and Freia must be surrendered. Despite the pleadings of his fellow immortals, Wotan refuses to give up the ring.

The stage suddenly darkens and Erda, the Earth goddess, rises from the depths. She warns Wotan that Alberich's curse will bring him disaster, and the god hurls the ring onto the pile of gold. The giants release Freia and start to divide their spoils between themselves. Immediately, the curse takes its deadly effect. Fasolt claims that Fafner is cheating him and, on Loge's advice, insists that his brother surrender the ring to him. Fafner snatches up his huge club and beats his brother to death in front of the horrified gods before taking ring, tarnhelm and treasure away. Loge congratulates Wotan

on his good fortune, but even Fricka's blandishments cannot relieve his dark mood – he, too, is now cursed.

Donner climbs to the top of a lofty rock. Summoning the storm clouds to him, he strikes the rock a mighty blow with his sturdy hammer. A lightning flash and clap of thunder follow. The clouds clear to reveal a rainbow bridge spanning the valley to Valhalla, which can now be seen clearly in the setting sun. Wotan hails the gods' new abode and, taking his wife by the hand, he calls on the gods to follow him in procession into the castle. Suddenly, Wotan pauses, as a possible solution to the day's ills comes into his mind: the creation of a race of demigods who will put an end to the Nibelung threat.

As the procession resumes, the voices of the Rhinemaidens are heard, still bewailing the loss of the Rhinegold. Wotan orders Loge to tell them to be silent – the gods are now their protectors – but the Rhinemaidens are not to be consoled. Although Valhalla's splendours are apparent, Wotan's power has been tainted by his possession of the ring.

Der Ring des Nibelungen

DIE WALKÜRE

Music-drama in three acts

CAST

Siegmund
Tenor

Sieglinde
his sister
Soprano

Hunding
her husband
Bass

Wotan
Baritone

Brünnhilde
his favourite
daughter
Soprano

Fricka
Wotan's wife
Mezzo-soprano

**The eight
Valkyries**
*Three sopranos, four
mezzo-sopranos, one
contralto*

LEFT The tragic Siegmund and Sieglinde not only fall in love but also discover that they are brother and sister. Their father, Walse, was Wotan in disguise.

BELOW Brünnhilde, Wotan's favourite child, greets her father with a wild war-cry. She is the leader of the Valkyries, bring the bodies of fallen heroes to Valhalla.

ACT ONE The interior of Hunding's hut. The orchestra conjures up the picture of a violent storm, which reaches its climax as the curtain rises and Siegmund staggers onto the scene and collapses on the hut floor. A beautiful young woman appears. She has heard someone arriving and, thinking it is her husband, Hunding, has hastened to greet him, although her haste is inspired by fear rather than love, for Hunding, in the absence of her father and kinsmen, had forcibly abducted and married her.

Strange feelings overcome Sieglinde as she bends over the fugitive. Suddenly, he calls for water and she snatches up a drinking-horn and hands it to him. As Siegmund drinks, he gazes at Sieglinde, who questioningly returns his gaze. He asks whose home this is and whether a weaponless stranger can beg shelter for the night. Sieglinde says he must await Hunding's return. She offers him mead, which the two drink, but Siegmund suddenly exclaims that he is a bringer of bad luck and must leave. Sieglinde begs him to stay, for he cannot bring sorrow to a home where sorrow already reigns.

The grim Hunding now enters. Sieglinde explains how she discovered this stranger unconscious on the threshold, and her husband bids her to prepare a meal. He starts to question

Siegmund, asking his name and how he came to arrive at the hut in such a state. Siegmund manages to avoid revealing the former but has no objection to explaining the latter. He grew up with his father, mother and twin sister deep in the forest. Returning from the hunt one day, he and his father found their hut in ashes, his mother dead and his sister vanished. Later, during a fight with their foes, he became separated from his father and ever since has wandered from place to place, misfortune following him. He has just come to the defence, for instance, of a girl whose brothers were trying to force into an unwanted marriage. However, when, in the fight that followed, he slew the girl's brothers while trying to protect her, she denounced him as a murderer and, ever since, he has been fleeing from her kinsmen, who are bent on revenge.

Hunding's face has turned darker and darker, and he reveals that the men Siegmund slew were his kinsmen. The laws of hospitality protect him for the night, but, in the morning, the two men must fight to the death. He orders Sieglinde to bed and the two leave Siegmund alone with his thoughts by the fireside. Suddenly, as he wonders where he can find the sword that his father promised would be his in his hour of need, he catches sight of a sword hilt, the blade of which is buried in the ash tree supporting the roof of the hut. Can this be the sword his father promised him?

At that moment, Sieglinde steals back into the hut. She has given her husband a sleeping potion and is hastening to tell Siegmund the story of the sword. On her wedding day, as Hunding and his kinsmen were feasting, a stranger entered and thrust a sword deep into the trunk of the tree. Try as they might, Hunding and his companions could not work the sword free. Only a true hero could be successful, and she is convinced that Siegmund is the chosen one. As the two embrace, the doors of the hut fly open and the scene is bathed in moonlight. It is the spring, says Siegmund, banishing winter.

They eagerly question each other. The man who thrust the sword into the ash was a Walsung, says Sieglinde, one of her own race. Siegmund starts. He, too, is a Walsung, and his father was none other than Walse himself. In triumph, he pulls the sword, which he christens Notung, from the tree as Sieglinde gasps that she is his long-lost sister. He has won her, along with the sword.

RIGHT Wotan reveals to Brünnhilde the trap into which he has fallen. His intention was that Siegmund should recover the ring and restore it to the Rhinemaidens, so lifting Alberich's curse, but this would mean breaking the sacred laws of contract he is pledged to uphold. Brünnhilde must, therefore, fight for Hunding, Sieglinde's husband, rather than for Siegmund as the two men battle to the death.

ACT TWO Wotan and Brünnhilde are discovered together on a rocky mountain. Wotan is giving his Valkyrie daughter her orders for the forthcoming fight between Siegmund and Hunding, in which she is to take Siegmund's side. She responds with an exultant battle cry, but, as she departs, she warns her father that Fricka is approaching, doubtless to upbraid him for this decision, since she is the protectress of sacred marriage vows.

This, indeed, is Fricka's mission. She demands vengeance on the incestuous Walsungs in the name of the betrayed Hunding. Wotan counters by explaining his plan in fathering this new race. Siegmund, he says, is an independent agent and, by returning the ring to the Rhinemaidens, he will lift the threat of Alberich's curse from the gods. To this, however, Fricka has a grimly logical counterargument. How can Siegmund be truly independent, when Brünnhilde is intervening at Wotan's behest? More than this, if the impious Walsungs are not punished, the gods themselves will be held up to the scorn of mankind and their fall will follow. Wotan twists and turns, but in vain. As Brünnhilde is heard returning, Fricka extracts from

LEFT Having punished Brünnhilde for her disobedience by kissing away her immortality and putting her to sleep, Wotan summons Loge, the god of fire, to ring her rock with protective flames. Only a man who has never known fear will be able to penetrate the barrier and awaken her.

him the promise that Hunding will be triumphant and that Siegmund will perish.

Brünnhilde, recognizing her father's misery, hurries to comfort him. Wotan explains what has brought him to this pass, how his plans to correct the situation have been thwarted and how the race of gods is doomed to oblivion. Alberich has won. In a passage of biting mockery, Wotan blesses the dwarf's heir, for he, too, has fostered a son on whom he depends to achieve his revenge. Brünnhilde is now to protect Hunding, as law, custom and contract command. He leaves, followed by Brünnhilde after she has sadly gathered her weapons.

Siegmund and Sieglinde enter, the latter in a state of collapse, while the horns signal Hunding's pursuit. She sinks to the ground, unconscious, as Siegmund vainly tries to comfort her. He looks up to see Brünnhilde standing before him. She tells him that he is to die and that she will carry him to

Valhalla, where he will be reunited with his father and join the other heroes she and her sister Valkyries have carried there to protect the gods. Siegmund has one question – will Sieglinde be there to greet him? Learning that she will not, he says he will slay her himself first, before he perishes. Brünnhilde, moved by Siegmund's heroism and obvious love, pledges that she will disobey Wotan – the two shall live and Hunding shall die.

Hunding's voice is heard, challenging Siegmund, who goes off to meet him, and Brünnhilde vanishes, as Sieglinde wakens. Alone and terrified, she witnesses the men's fight. Brünnhilde protects Siegmund with her shield, but, as he is poised to strike Hunding to the heart, Wotan appears. He interposes his sacred spear between the two combatants and Notung shatters. Hunding thrusts his spear into the defenceless Siegmund's breast. With a wild shriek, Sieglinde falls to the ground, but is rescued by Brünnhilde who, taking also the

Der Ring des Nibelungen

SIEGFRIED

Music-drama in three acts

pieces of Notung, carries her off to the Valkyries' rock.

Hunding and Wotan stand for a moment in silence. Wotan bids him take the news to Fricka and makes a contemptuous gesture with his spear. Hunding falls dead. Gathering himself together, the god swears vengeance on Brünnhilde for her disobedience and sets off in hot pursuit.

ACT THREE The Valkyrie rock. The Valkyries are gathering, each with a slain hero, ready to take them on to Valhalla. Suddenly, Brünnhilde is sighted, riding through the clouds with a woman, rather than a hero, slung over her saddle. She tells her sisters what has happened, of how Wotan is hot on her heels and begs them to lend her a fresh horse. They are too terrified of the god's wrath to help her.

As the gathering thunderclouds herald Wotan's approach, Brünnhilde turns to Sieglinde. She will stay and brave her father's fury, but Sieglinde must take flight on her own and look for shelter in the nearby forest. When Sieglinde protests that she would rather die, so that she may be reunited with Siegmund, the Valkyrie tells her that she has a more important destiny to fulfil. She is to bear Siegmund's son, Siegfried, the hero who will finally put an end to Alberich's curse. Sieglinde hurries off into the dark.

Wotan arrives on the rock to confront Brünnhilde, whose sisters have grouped themselves around her to protect her. She pleads with him to pardon her, but he has already decided on her punishment. He will put her to sleep, unprotected, on the rock, and the first man who kisses her awake, whoever he may be, shall remove her immortality. Horrorstruck, the Valkyries flee, leaving father and daughter alone.

Brünnhilde kneels in penitence at Wotan's feet and renews her plea. In a last appeal, she tells Wotan, whose anger is already being replaced by grief, that Sieglinde is to give birth to Siegfried, the hero for whom her father has been waiting. She will accept her fate, but she implores Wotan to surround her with a circle of magic fire, which only a fearless hero will be able to penetrate. He agrees and bids her farewell. Having gently laid her on the rock and kissed her to sleep, he summons Loge, the god of fire. As tongues of flame surround the sleeping Brünnhilde, he makes his way sadly and alone into the night.

CAST

Mime
Tenor

Siegfried
Tenor

Wotan
disguised as the Wanderer
Baritone

Alberich
Bass-baritone

Fafner
transformed into a dragon
Bass

The wood bird
Soprano

Erda
Contralto

Brünnhilde
Soprano

ACT ONE Mime is discovered, hammering at a sword he is forging in his forest smithy. He is full of complaints – no matter how hard he tries, every sword he forges is broken by Siegfried, who lives with him. His only recourse would be to reforge the shards of Notung, but this is beyond his powers. At this moment, Siegfried bursts into the smithy, driving a bear before him, which he urges on to tease the terrified dwarf. When Mime reproaches him for his ingratitude, Siegfried questions him about who he is, from where he came and, refusing to accept Mime's assertion that he is Siegfried's father and mother in one, who his real parents might be. Eventually, Mime is forced to admit the truth. He found the youth as a baby lying by his dead mother's side in the forest, she having obviously perished in giving birth to him. To prove the truth of his words, the dwarf produces the shards of Notung, which he found at the same time.

Siegfried is overjoyed by this revelation. He orders Mime to reforge the sword at once. Once this has been accomplished, he will be able to leave his hated companion for ever. As he runs off

LEFT Siegfried triumphantly reforges the shards of Notung, the sword of his father, Siegmund, in the flames of Mime's smithy.

Der Ring des Nibelungen – Siegfried

RIGHT Grandson and grandfather meet as Siegfried and the Wanderer confront each other at the foot of Brünnhilde's rock. Learning that it was the Wanderer who was responsible for his father's death, Siegfried cuts through the shaft of his spear with the reforged Notung. The Wanderer, robbed of his power, vanishes.

into the forest, Mime sinks back into despair but is interrupted by the arrival of a majestic figure, hatted, cloaked and carrying a long spear. It is Wotan, disguised as the Wanderer. The two get into conversation and eventually embark on a riddling game, in which it is agreed that the loser shall forfeit his head. Mime poses three questions, all of which the Wanderer answers correctly. In his turn the dwarf gets his first two answers right, but is totally defeated by the third question: "Who will reforge Siegmund's sword?" The Wanderer leaves, assuring Mime that he will fall victim to the one who can accomplish the deed and that this will be someone who is totally ignorant of fear.

Mime grovels in terror. He seems to see Fafner, who has turned himself into a dragon by means of the tarnhelm, advancing on him and recoils in horror, just as Siegfried returns. Eagerly, the youth asks Mime how the reforging of Notung has progressed in his absence, but the dwarf has other things on his mind. He realizes that, in educating Siegfried, he had forgotten to teach him what fear means, and he promptly starts trying to rectify what he now realizes might be a fatal oversight. When he tells Siegfried of the dragon and the hoard he guards, however, the effect is completely the opposite of what he intended. Having wrung

from him the confession that he is incapable of reforging Notung, Siegfried snatches up the shards and gets down to the task himself.

As the forging proceeds, Mime anxiously watches. Suddenly, he sees a way out of his dilemma. Let Siegfried forge the sword and kill Fafner. The dwarf will persuade the young hero to drink poison once he has recovered the ring, tarnhelm and golden hoard. As Mime capers in glee, Siegfried triumphantly splits the smithy anvil in two with the newly reforged sword and the curtain falls.

ACT TWO Outside Fafner's forest lair. It is night. A ghostly figure is seen in the background. It is Alberich, who is haunting the cave that holds the treasures of which he was robbed. Wotan, still disguised as the Wanderer, tells the dwarf that Siegfried and Mime are approaching, and Alberich, seeking to take advantage of the situation, alerts Fafner to the coming danger. The sole reply is that food is near. The Wanderer departs and Alberich slips back into concealment.

Siegfried and Mime enter, the latter still trying to awaken Siegfried's sense of fear. But all his warnings serve only to arouse Siegfried's ardour,

Der Ring des Nibelungen – Siegfried

RIGHT Siegfried kisses Brünnhilde awake. The two hail the light and their newly kindled love.

and eventually he angrily drives Mime away. Resting under a tree, Siegfried muses on his mother and wonders what she was like. The sound of a bird's voice is heard and he tries to imitate it with a reed pipe. Having failed with this, he picks up his hunting horn and soon the forest rings with its call. The noise reawakens Fafner, who crawls forth into the attack. A brief fight follows, which ends when Siegfried plunges Notung deep into the dragon's heart.

Licking the dragon's blood from his fingers, Siegfried looks about him. The wood bird's voice is heard again, but, this time, the young hero can understand every word that is being sung. The wood bird tells him of the ring, tarnhelm and other treasures in Fafner's cave, and he disappears in search of them, just as Mime and Alberich re-enter. The two dwarfs immediately start to quarrel, a dispute interrupted by Siegfried's return, when Alberich again conceals himself.

The wood bird counsels Siegfried to beware of Mime, who approaches, the flask of poisoned drink in his hand. Siegfried's newly acquired magic powers enable him to fathom the true meaning of everything Mime sings and, enraged by his duplicity, he slays the dwarf. As Mime perishes, Alberich's mocking laugh is heard.

The wood bird has one more task to fulfil. As Siegfried rests under the tree, it sings of Brünnhilde and how the circle of fire that guards her can be penetrated only by a fearless hero. Siegfried exultantly follows the wood bird in the direction of Brünnhilde's rock.

ACT THREE A stormy prelude sets the scene for the opening of the last act of the opera, at the foot of Brünnhilde's rock. Wotan enters and summons Erda, the Earth goddess, from her slumbers. He anxiously seeks her counsel for the future, but she replies that she has no advice to offer. Eventually, he renounces his rule and that of the other gods in favour of a new era, which, founded on human love, might mean a new beginning for the world and an end to the Nibelung curse. Siegfried, still following the wood bird, enters. Wotan, as the

rock's defender, challenges him. Siegfried must force his way past him before he can reach his prize. He reveals that the spear he is holding is the very weapon that shattered Notung once before in the past, and the young hero hurls himself on the figure whom he supposes was his father's murderer. Wotan's spear is broken, and the god vanishes. Blowing his horn, Siegfried makes his way up through the flames.

As Siegfried reaches the mountain top, the flames die down. Brünnhilde, in full armour, is revealed in deep slumber. Siegfried approaches her and starts back in wonder as he releases the sleeping Valkyrie from her armour. Gently, he kisses her awake. Brünnhilde reawakens and salutes the world and the hero who has awoken her. At first she hesitates, for, by giving in to her growing emotions, she will surrender her last remnants of immortality, but Siegfried's ardour rouses similar passion in her. A triumphant duet between the two ends as they rush off into Brünnhilde's cave.

Der Ring des Nibelungen

GÖTTERDÄMMERUNG

Music-drama in a prologue and three acts

CAST

The Norns
Contralto, mezzo-soprano, soprano

Brünnhilde
Soprano

Siegfried
Tenor

Gunther
Baritone

Hagen
Gunther's half-brother and Alberich's son
Bass

Gutrune
Soprano

Waltraute
Mezzo-soprano

Alberich
Bass-baritone

Woglinde, Wellgunde and Flosshilde
the Rhinemaidens
Soprano, soprano, contralto

Chorus
Vassals and women

LEFT **The Gibichung vassals gather in Act Two to celebrate the wedding of Gutrune and Siegfried and the betrothal of Gunther and Brünnhilde. Urged on by Hagen, Gunther and Brünhilde swear to take revenge on Siegfried for his apparent perfidy.**

PROLOGUE The curtain rises on Brünnhilde's rock. The scene is the same as at the close of *Siegfried*, with firelight still flickering around the rock. The three Norns, daughters of the goddess Erda, are discovered, spinning the rope of destiny, which stretches between them across the stage.

The first Norn tells how Wotan came to the spring beneath the world ash tree and sacrificed one of his eyes in order to drink from it to earn wisdom and how he broke a branch from the tree with which to shape his magic spear. The wound slowly weakened the tree and the spring failed. The second and third Norns take up the story. When Siegfried broke the spear, Wotan ordered the world ash to be cut down and the faggots heaped around Valhalla. When Wotan summons Loge, the god of fire, both the gods and the dead heroes, whom the Valkyries brought to protect

Valhalla, will perish and the world will come to an end. The Norns suddenly realize that the rope of destiny is fraying, affected by the power of Alberich's curse. It snaps. The Norns start up in terror and gather at the centre of the stage, holding the pieces of the rope. Proclaiming that their wisdom has come to an end and they must return to their mother, they vanish.

Dawn breaks, the firelight grows fainter, and, as the sun starts to shine, Brünnhilde and Siegfried emerge from the cave in which they have spent the night. They celebrate their new-found love in an ecstatic duet and, to mark their union, Siegfried gives Brünnhilde the ring. In return, she presents him with Grane, her horse, to carry him away to new adventures. Siegfried leaves and, as his horn call is heard, the curtain falls.

RIGHT The three Norns anxiously confer at the start of the prologue. When the rope of fate snaps, it is the signal that the time of the gods is over and they descend into the bowels of the earth to rejoin Erda, their mother.

ORCHESTRAL INTERLUDE

SIEGFRIED'S RHINE JOURNEY

Here Wagner conjures up in music the sound of horse and rider on their journey, culminating in a crescendo of sound as they plunge into the River Rhine. The mood darkens as the curtain rises on the first scene of Act 1 proper.

ACT ONE
SCENE 1
In the hall of the Gibichungs, one of the human tribes that have settled along the banks of the Rhine, Gunther is seated on one throne and his sister, Gutrune, on another. Before them stands their half-brother, Hagen. Gunther questions Hagen about his power and prestige, and Hagen replies that the problem is that both Gunther and his sister are unmarried. Brünnhilde would be the ideal bride, if Siegfried could be made to win her for Gunther and, at the same time, marry Gutrune. He will give Siegfried a magic potion to drink, which (though Hagen does not reveal this fact) will make him forget the past and, at the same time, make him fall hopelessly in love with Gutrune. Both Gunther and Gutrune applaud the scheme. As they ask how they can lure Siegfried to the hall, his horn is heard off-stage, swiftly followed by his entrance.

While Gutrune withdraws to prepare the magic potion as Hagen has directed, the three men talk. Hagen asks Siegfried about his adventures and his combat with Fafner. The hero replies that he left the golden hoard behind, having removed only a ring, which he has left with a woman for safe-keeping, and a curious helmet, which is hanging at his waist. Hagen recognizes the tarnhelm and tells of its magical powers.

Gutrune re-enters, bearing the magic potion. As Siegfried drains it, his whole manner alters. Eagerly, he questions Gunther about her and the two men eventually agree on a bargain. Using the tarnhelm as a disguise, Siegfried will penetrate the magic flames and bring back Brünnhilde for

Gunther. In return, Gunther will give him Gutrune as his wife. The three men swear an oath of blood brotherhood, and Siegfried and Gunther leave on their journey back to the rock. Hagen is left to brood over the success of his plot.

ACT ONE
SCENE 2
A brief orchestral interlude takes us back to Brünnhilde, who is sitting thinking of Siegfried and her love for him. Suddenly, her musing is interrupted by the sound of a Valkyrie horse. Waltraute, one of Brünnhilde's warrior sisters, enters. She tells how Wotan and his fellow gods are assembled in Valhalla, awaiting their end. Only one thing can save them – Brünnhilde must return the ring to the Rhinemaidens and so lift Alberich's curse. She refuses to give up the token of Siegfried's love, and the despairing Valkyrie gallops off into the gathering dusk.

As the stage darkens, the magic flames begin to rise again. The notes of Siegfried's horn are heard, and Brünnhilde rushes joyously to greet her lover, falling back in dismay when a stranger makes his way onto the scene. Siegfried has donned the tarnhelm and now appears in the form of Gunther. As Brünnhilde tries to use the power of the ring to protect herself, he tears it from her finger and orders her into the cave. Drawing Notung from its scabbard, Siegfried swears that it will lie between him and his future brother-in-law's wife for the night.

Der Ring des Nibelungen – Götterdämmerung

`ACT TWO` Outside the Gibichung hall, Hagen is sitting alone on watch, half-dreaming. Suddenly, Alberich is at his side, urging him to murder Siegfried and seize the ring. Hagen assures Alberich that he will be true to his oath, and the Nibelung vanishes as day dawns. Siegfried returns, wearing the ring. Gunther and Brünnhilde are following, he says, and Hagen should at once rouse the Gibichung vassals and bid them prepare for the double betrothal that is to follow.

Hagen rouses the vassals with a loud horn call. They are quick to assemble, ready to fight at their lord's command, but Hagen tells them that it is a wedding they will be celebrating. They hail Gunther and his bride, but, as Siegfried and Guntrune re-enter, Brünnhilde starts in amazement, her eyes caught by the ring. She asks Gunther how and why he gave the ring he wrestled from her to Siegfried and, when the Gibichung denies all knowledge of the incident, angrily tells him that both he and she have been betrayed by the perfidious Siegfried. The latter indignantly denies the charge, swearing on the point of Hagen's spear that, if he has played Gunther false, may he perish at the spear point. Brünnhilde blesses the spear that will retrieve her lost honour.

Siegfried, still nonplussed by what has occurred, tells Gunther to tend his obviously distraught bride, and the wedding party moves into the hall, leaving Brünnhilde, Gunther and Hagen alone. Brünnhilde is determined on vengeance, Gunther is now suspicious that her accusations are true, and Hagen is determined to win the ring. At his prompting, the three swear that Siegfried shall die during the hunt the next day, as the wedding party joyfully returns.

`ACT THREE` By the banks of the Rhine Siegfried discovers the three Rhine-
`SCENE 1` maidens swimming. They beg him to give them back the ring, but, when he refuses, they leave him to his fate. Distant horn calls herald the arrival of the rest of the hunting party. Hagen suggests to Siegfried that he tell the assembled company the story of his life but, as he pauses halfway through his narrative, urges him to quench his thirst from a drinking horn, into which he has poured a second magic potion. This restores Siegfried's memory up to the moment he wooed and won Brünnhilde. Gunther starts up – Brünnhilde's accusation was true.

Hagen asks Siegfried, as he understands the language of birds, what the two ravens that are passing overhead are saying. As he turns his back on Hagen to look at them, the Gibichung plunges his spear into Siegfried's back. He falls dying, as the horrified Gibichungs cower in the shadows. As Hagen stalks off, Gunther and his followers listen to Siegfried's death-song.

`ORCHESTRAL INTERLUDE`

SIEGFRIED'S FUNERAL MARCH

As the orchestra launches a funeral march, the vassals lift Siegfried's corpse onto their shoulders and slowly make their way back to the hall.

`ACT THREE` The Gibichung hall. Gutrune
`SCENE 2` enters, fearing that some evil has befallen her newly wed husband for she was aroused from sleep by the sound of Brünnhilde's laughter in the adjoining room. Her fears are all too quickly confirmed as Hagen enters, bringing the news of Siegfried's death. As the funeral party enters with the corpse, she rounds on her brother, who is overcome with remorse. Hagen grimly demands the ring as his share of the spoils, but Gunther moves to prevent him. Drawing his sword, Hagen slays Gunther and is about to seize the ring when, miraculously, the dead hero's arm rises in warning. Brünnhilde advances. She has learned from the Rhinemaidens of Hagen's treachery and orders the vassals to build a funeral pyre. Singing a passionate greeting to her dead lover and a farewell to the race of gods, she kindles the flames. Bidding the ravens carry the news of what has happened to Valhalla, she places the ring on her finger and joins her lover on the blazing pyre.

The Rhine bursts its banks and pours into the hall, carrying the Rhinemaidens with it. As Hagen makes a last desperate attempt to seize the ring, he is carried off by two of them in the flood, while the third holds the ring above her head in triumph. As the flood starts to subside, a deep glow is seen in the skies. Valhalla burns. A musical motif – heard only once before in the entire cycle in Act 3 of *Die Walküre* at Sieglinde's final exit – is heard again. It is the motif of redemption. Through Brünnhilde's self-sacrifice the curse of the ring has been lifted and a new age is dawning, an age that will recognize the power of human love.

INDEX

ACKNOWLEDGEMENTS

Photographs reproduced by kind permission of the following:

REX FEATURES p8, 9, 11.

Winnie Klotz at the Metropolitan Opera Association
p13, 14, 16, 18 b, 19, 20 l, 21, 23, 25, 26, 27, 29, 30, 33, 35 tl, b, 38, 41, 42, 43, 44, 45 t, 46, 49b, 51, 52t, 53, 55, 56, 57, 59, 60, 61, 62, 63, 65b, 69, 75, 76, 78, 79, 80–100, 102b, 104b, 105, 107, 108, 109, 110b, 113, 115, 117, 118, 119, 120, 121, 122, 123, 124, 125.

William Rafferty at the English National Opera
p18t, 20r, 31, 35tr, 36, 37, 39, 40, 43r, 45b, 47, 48, 49t, 50, 52b, 64, 65t, 66, 67, 71, 72, 73, 101, 102t, 103, 104t, 110t, 111, 112

The singers
14 Hildegarde Behrens (Leonora), Reiner Goldberg (Florestan); 16 Monserrat Caballe (Norma), Shirley Verrett (Adalgisa); 18 top, Sally Burgess (Carmen), b Cheryl Studer (Micaela); 19 Agnes Baltsa (Carmen); 20 Agnes Baltsa (Carmen), Jose Carreras (Don Jose), r Sally Burgess (Carmen), Edmund Barham (Don Jose) Donald Maxwell (Escamillo); 21 Agnes Baltsa (Carmen) Jose Carreras (Don Jose); 23 June Anderson (Lucia); 26 Terry Cook (Porgy), Priscilla Baskerville (Bess); 27 Priscilla Baskerville (Bess), Greg Baker (Crown); 29 b Juan Pons (Tonio); 30 l Ermanno Mauro (Canio); 31 Rowland Sidewell (Canio), Helen Field (Nedda); 33 b Ghena Demetrova (Santuzza); 35 tl Helen Donath (Susana), Samuel Ramey (Figaro), tr Etha Robinson (Cherubino), Steven Page (Count Almaviva), Lesley Garrett (Susanna), b Thomas Hampson (Count Almaviva) Susanne Mentzer (Cherubino); 36 Etha Robinson (Cherubino), Lesley Garrett (Susanna), Valerie Masterson (Countess Almaviva); 37 Etha Robinson (Cherubino), Lesley Garrett (Susanna); 38 t Ferrucio Furlanetto (Figaro) 39 Linda McLeod (Donna Elvira), Arwel Hugh Morgan (Leporello); 40 t Peter Coleman-Wright (Don Giovanni), b Peter Coleman-Wright (Don Giovanni), Lesley Garrett (Zerlina); 41b Hans Blochwitz (Don Ottavio); 42 Ferrucio Furlanetto (Leporello), Samuel Ramey (Don Giovanni); 43 Peter Coleman-Wright (Don Giovanni), Brian Bannatyne-Scott (Commendatore); 45 t Marilyn Mims (Dorabella), b Etha Robinson (Dorabella); 46 l Hel-Kyung Hong (Despina), r Carol Vaness (Fiordiligi), David Rendall (Ferrando); 48 Paul Nilon (Tamino); 49t Alan Opie (Papageno), b Luciana Serra (Queen of Night); 50 Benjamin Luxon (Papageno), Cathryn Pope (Pamina); 51 l Francisco Araiza (Tamino), r Kurt Moll (Sarastro); 52t Francisco Araiza (Tamino), Kathleen Battle (Pamina), b Benjamin Luxon (Papageno); 55 b Paate Burchyuladze (Boris); 56 Paate Burchyuladze (Boris); 57 t Stefania Toczyska (Marina), Gary Lakes (Dmitri), b Paate Burchyuladze (Boris), Andrea Velis (Simpleton); 59 Gabriela Benackova (Mimi), Luis Lima (Rodolfo); 60 t Nancy Gustafson (Musetta), b Gabriela Benackova (Mimi), Dwayne Croft (Marcello); 61 t Luis Lima (Rodolfo), Dwayne Croft (Marcello), b Gabriela Benackova (Mimi), Luis Lima (Rodolfo), Nancy Gustafson (Musetta); 62 Ghena Dimitrova (Tosca), Luciano Pavarotti (Cavaradossi); 64 Jane Eaglen (Tosca), David Rendall (Cavaradossi); 65 t Josephine Barstow (Tosca); 66 Arthur Davies (Pinkerton), Susan Bullock (Butterfly); 67 Alan Opie (Sharpless), Susan Bullock (Butterfly); 69 t Gwyneth Jones (Turandot), b Teresa Stratas (Liù); 71 Thomas Hampson (Figaro); 73 Thomas Hampson (Figaro), Gabriel Bacquier (Doctor Bartolo); 75 Pamela Koburn (Rosalinda), Siegfried Jerusalem (Eisenstein); 76 l Pamela Koburn (Rosalinda); 78 l Aage Haugland (Baron Ochs), r Stanford Olson; 79 b Anne Sophie von Otter (Sophie); 80 Felicity Lott (Marschallin); 82 b Richard Leech (Duke of Mantus); 83 Matteo Manuerra (Rigoletta); 84 l Matteo Manuerra (Rigoletto), Ruth Ann Swenson (Gilda), r Matteo Manuerra (Rigoletto), Ruth Ann Swenson (Gilda), Richard Leech (Duke of Mantus); 85 Susan Dunn (Leonora); 86 l Susan Dunn (Leonora), Ermanno Mauro (Manrico), r Shirley Verrett (Azucena), Ermanno Mauro (Manrico); 87 Susan Dunn (Leonora); 88 Ermanno Mauro (Manrico); 89 Marilyn Mims (Violetta), Jerry Hadley (Alfredo); 90 tl Marilyn Mims (Violetta), Jerry Hadley (Alfredo), tr Jerry Hadley (Alfredo), b Marilyn Mims (Violetta); 91 Marilyn Mims (Violetta), Brian Scheynayder (Germont), b Marilyn Mims (Violetta), Brian Scheynayder (Germont); 93 Vladimir Popov (Radames);95 Aprile Millo (Aida), Barseq Tumayan (Amonasro); 96 Aprile Millo (Aida), Barseq Tumayan (Amonasro), Vladimir Popov (Radames); 98 l Placido Domingo (Otello), r Sherrill Milnes (Iogo);99 t Placido Domingo (Otello), Gilda Cruz-Romo (Desdemona), b Placido Domingo (Otello); 100 t Sherrill Milnes (Iago), Placido Domingo (Otello), b Gilda Cruz-Romo (Desdemona); 101 Benjamin Luxon (Falstaff), Edward Byles (Bardolph), Richard Angas (Pistol); 102 t Susan Bullock (Alice Ford), Anne Collin (Mistress Quickly), b Frank Lopardo (Fenton), Barbara Bonney (Nannetta); 103 Benjamin Luxon (Falstaff); 104 t Susan Bullock (Alice Ford), Benjamin Luxon (Falstaff), b Paul Plishka (Falstaff), Susan Graham (Mistress Page); 105 l Paul Plishka (Falstaff), r Barbara Bonney (Nanetta); 107 t Hildegarde Behrens (Isolde), b Hildegarde Behrens (Isolde), Manfred Jung (Tristan); 108 Manfred Jung (Tristan), r Hildegarde Behrens (Isolde); 110 t Gwynne Howell (Hans Sachs) Alberto Remidios (Walther von Stolzing); 112 Peter Hoffman (Walther);113 l Alan Opie (Beckmesser); 118 l Gary Lakes (Siegmund), Jessye Norman (Sieglinde), r Gwyneth Jones (Brunnhilde); 119 James Morris (Wotan), Gwyneth Jones (Brunnhilde); 121 Siegfried Jerusalem (Siegfried); 122 Siegfried Jerusalem (Siegfried); 123 Siegfried Jerusalem (Siegfried), Hildegarde Behrens (Brunnhilde).

Every effort has been made to identify singers.